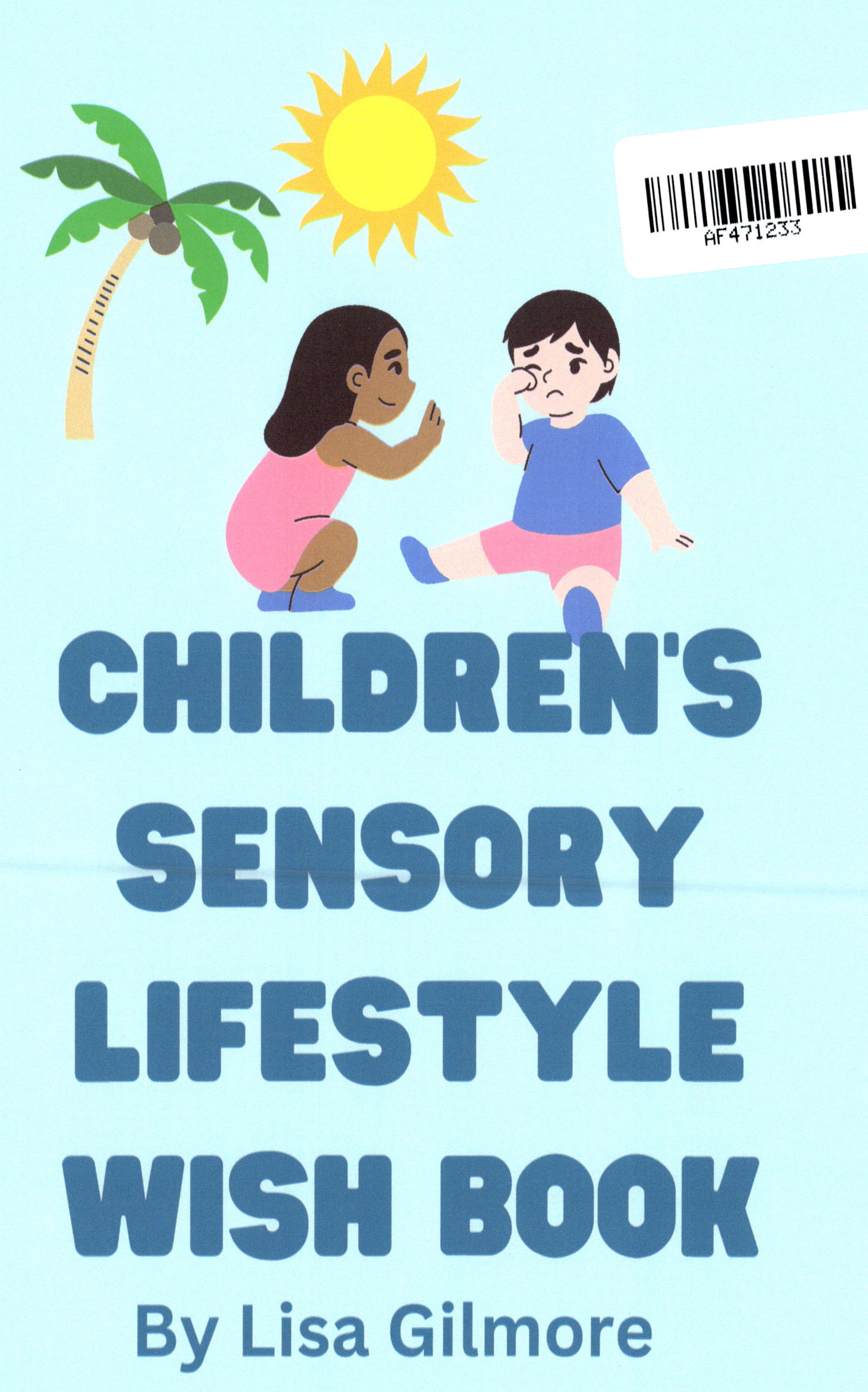

CHILDREN'S SENSORY LIFESTYLE WISH BOOK

By Lisa Gilmore

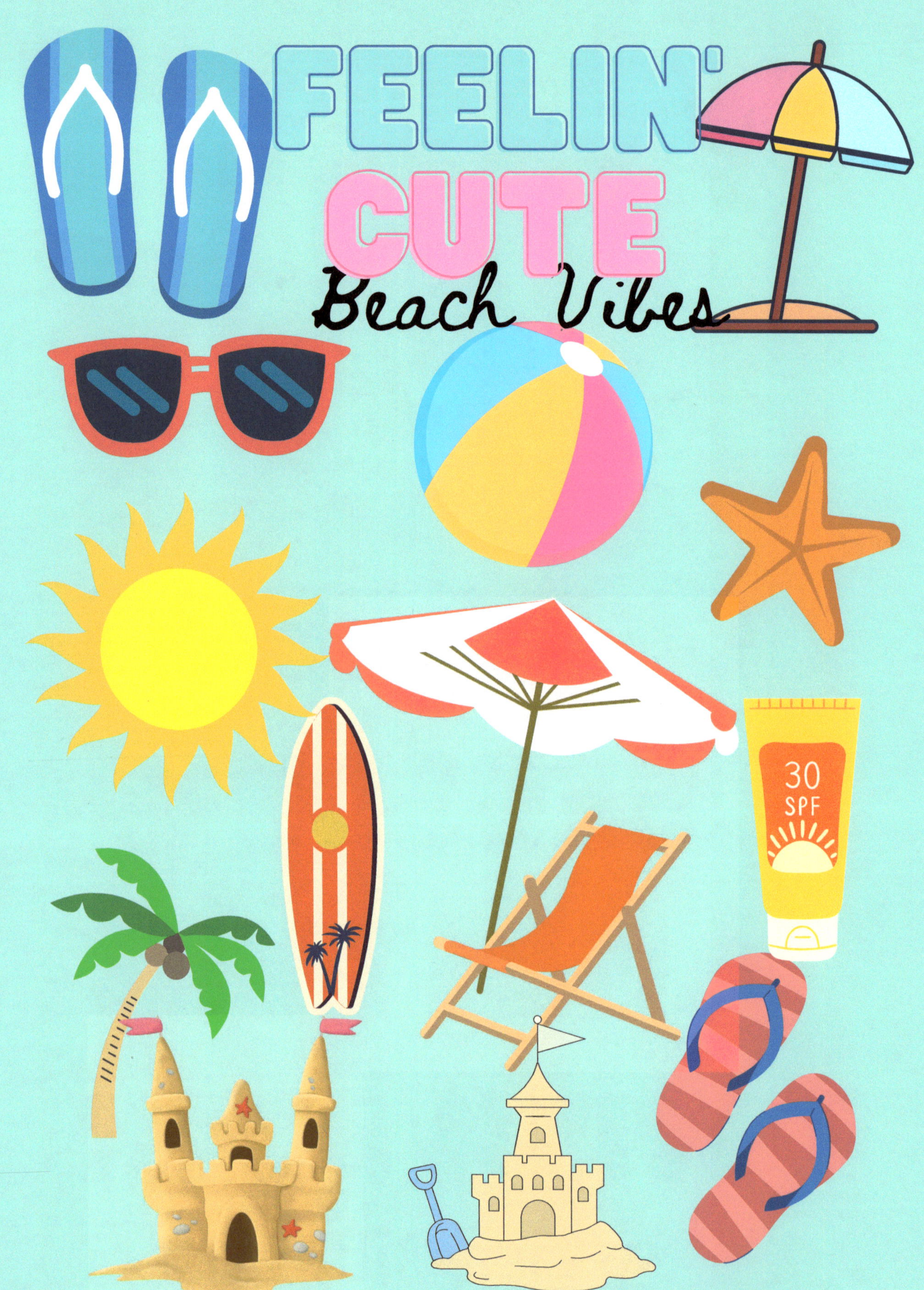

FEELIN'
CUTE
Beach Vibes
30 SPF

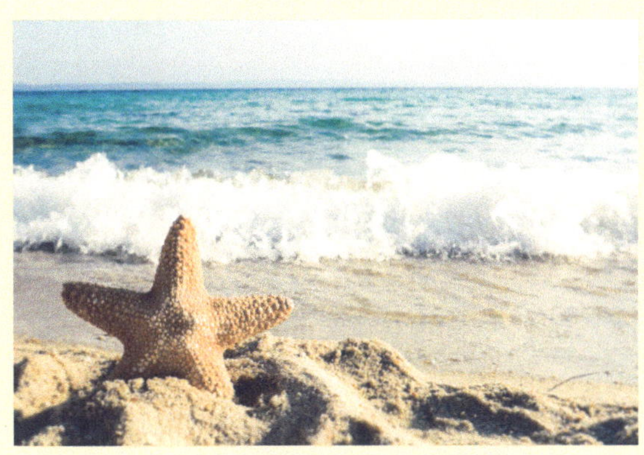

SHELLS

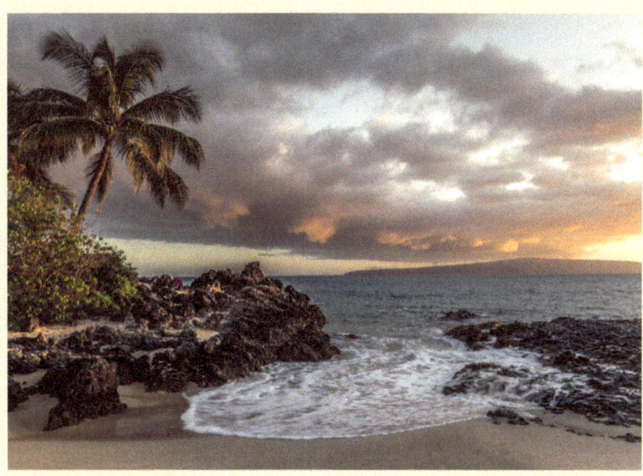

SAND

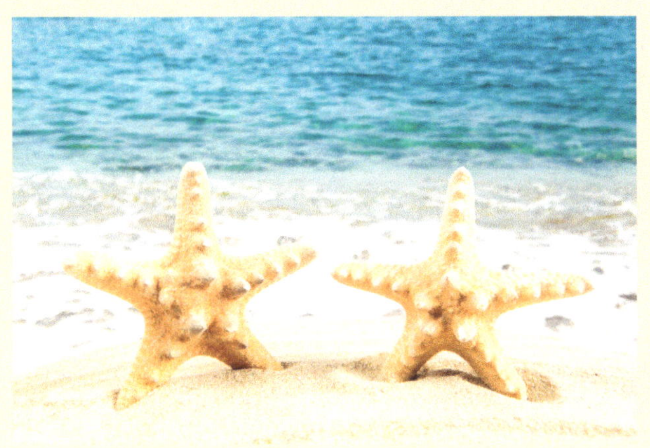

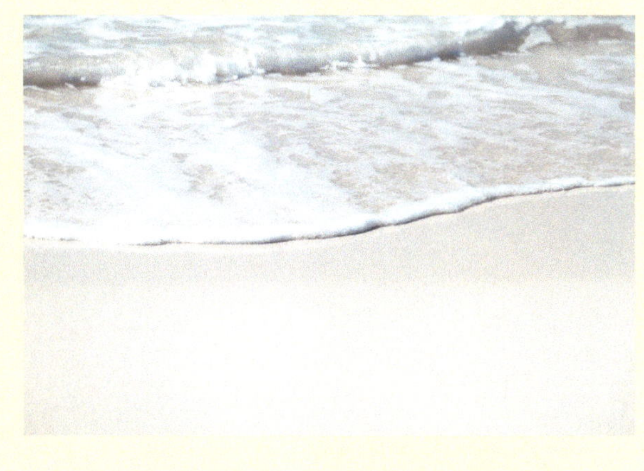

BEACHES

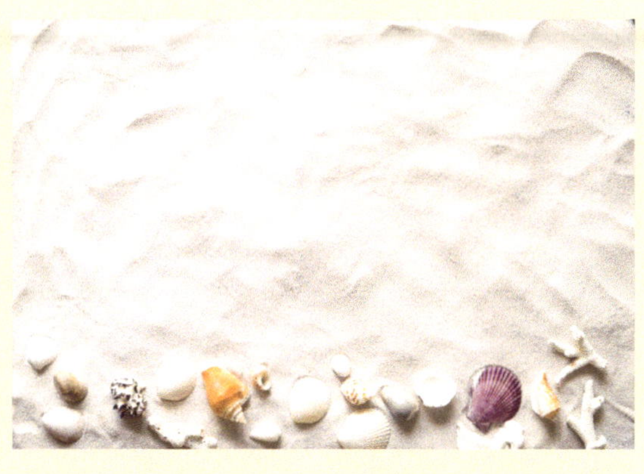

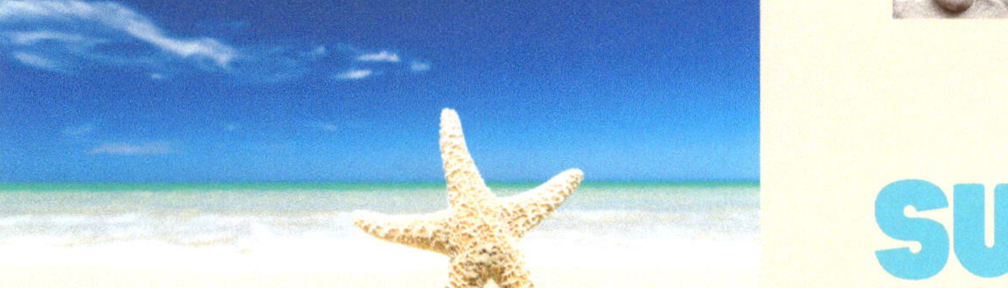

SURF TIME

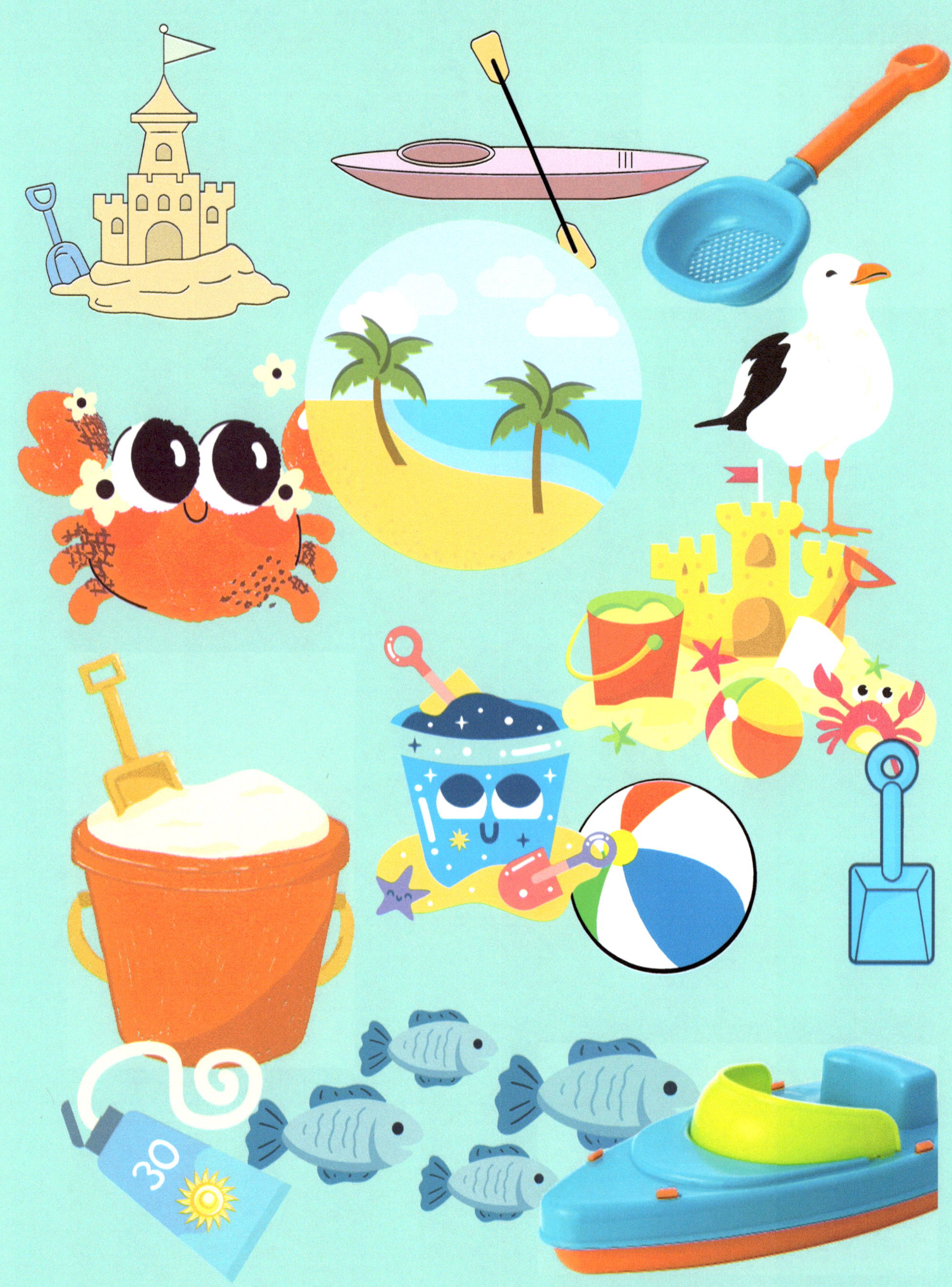

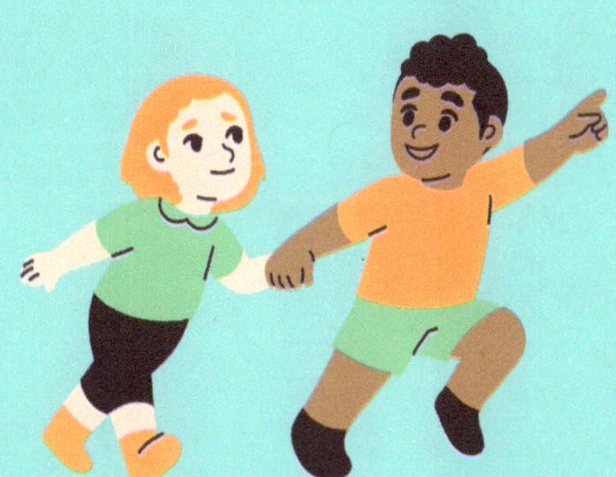

friends

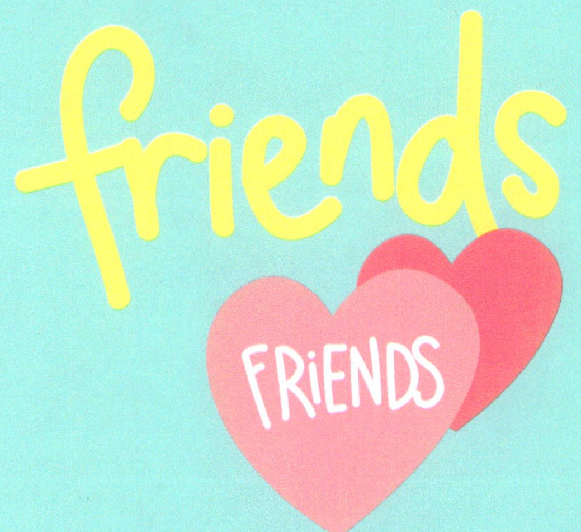

FRiENDS

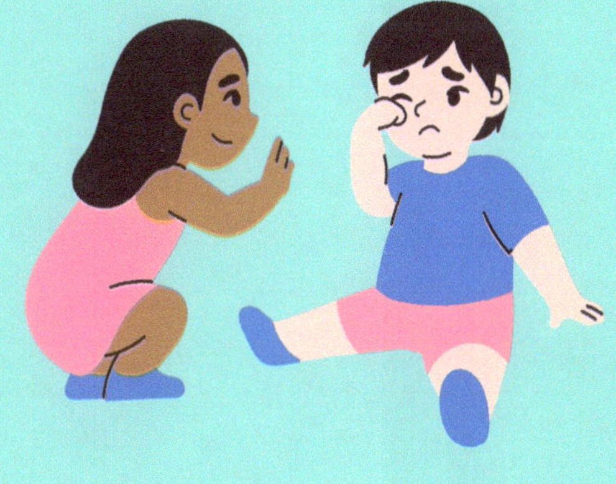

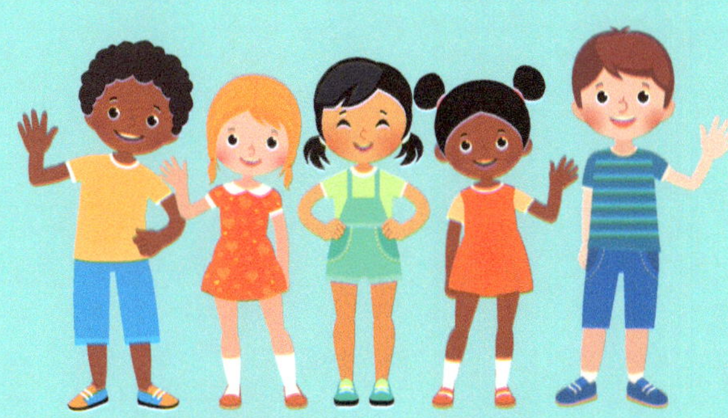

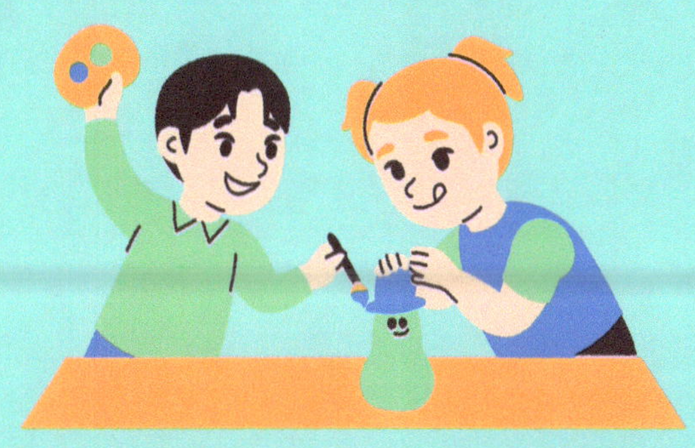

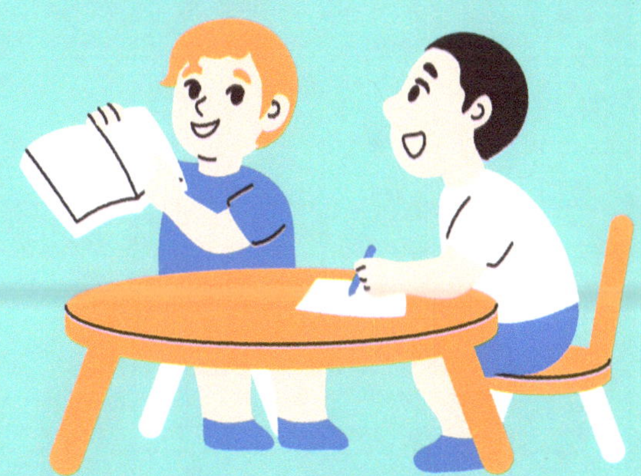

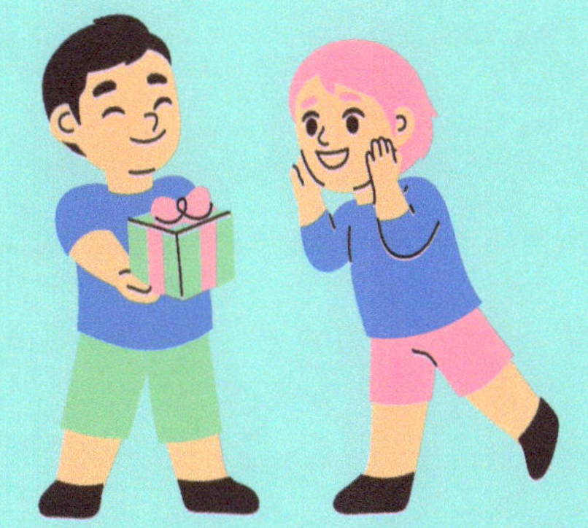

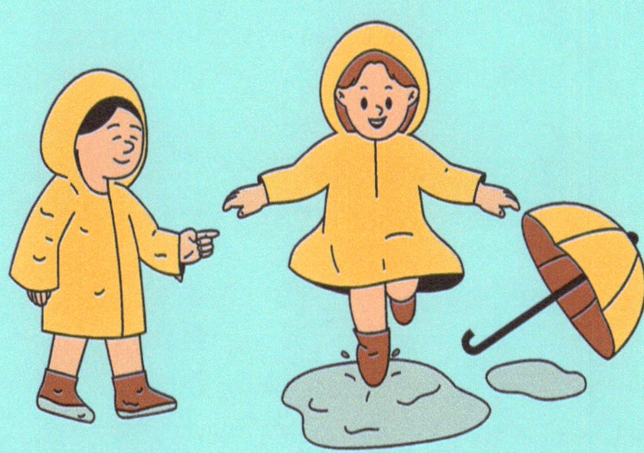

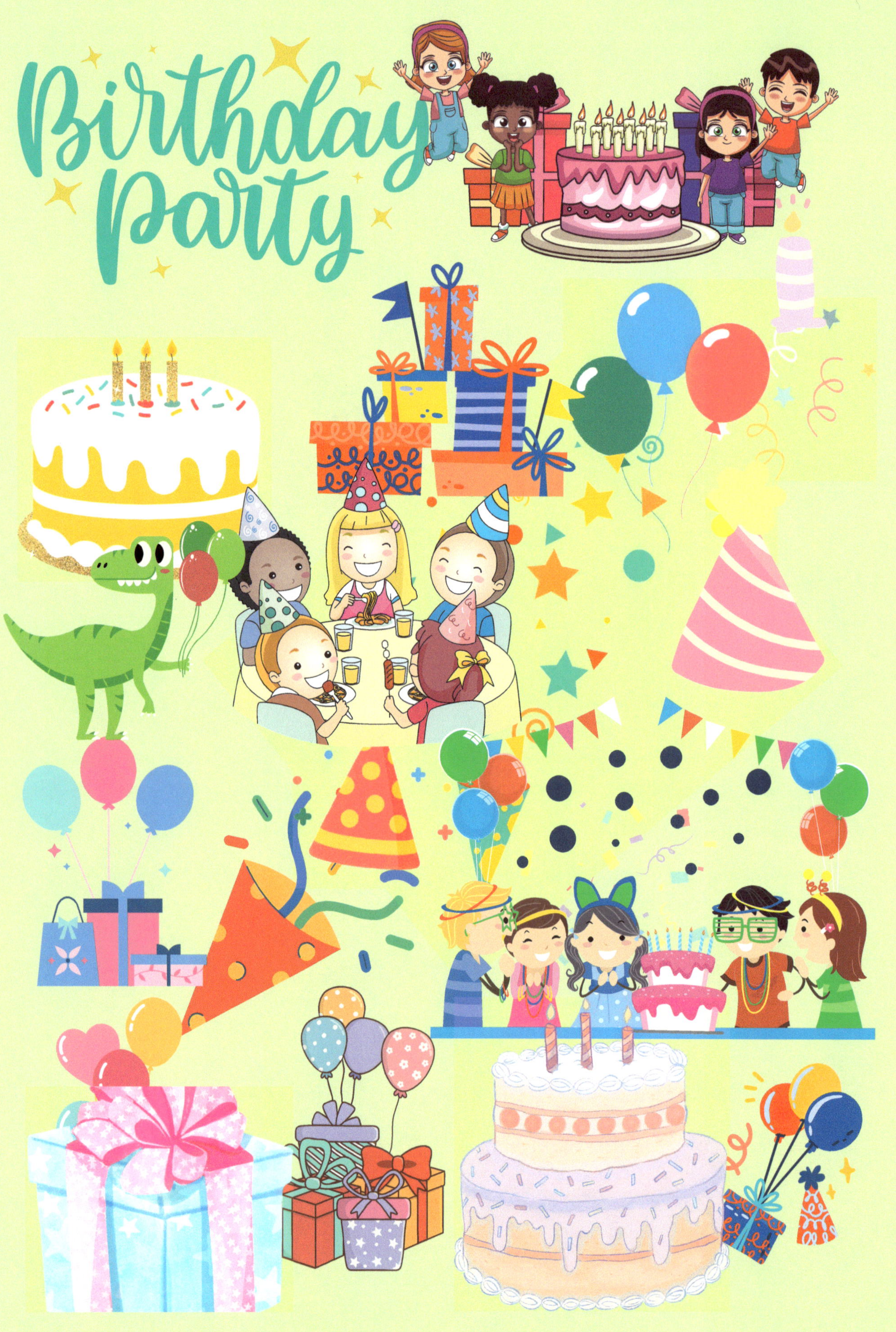

Birthday
Party

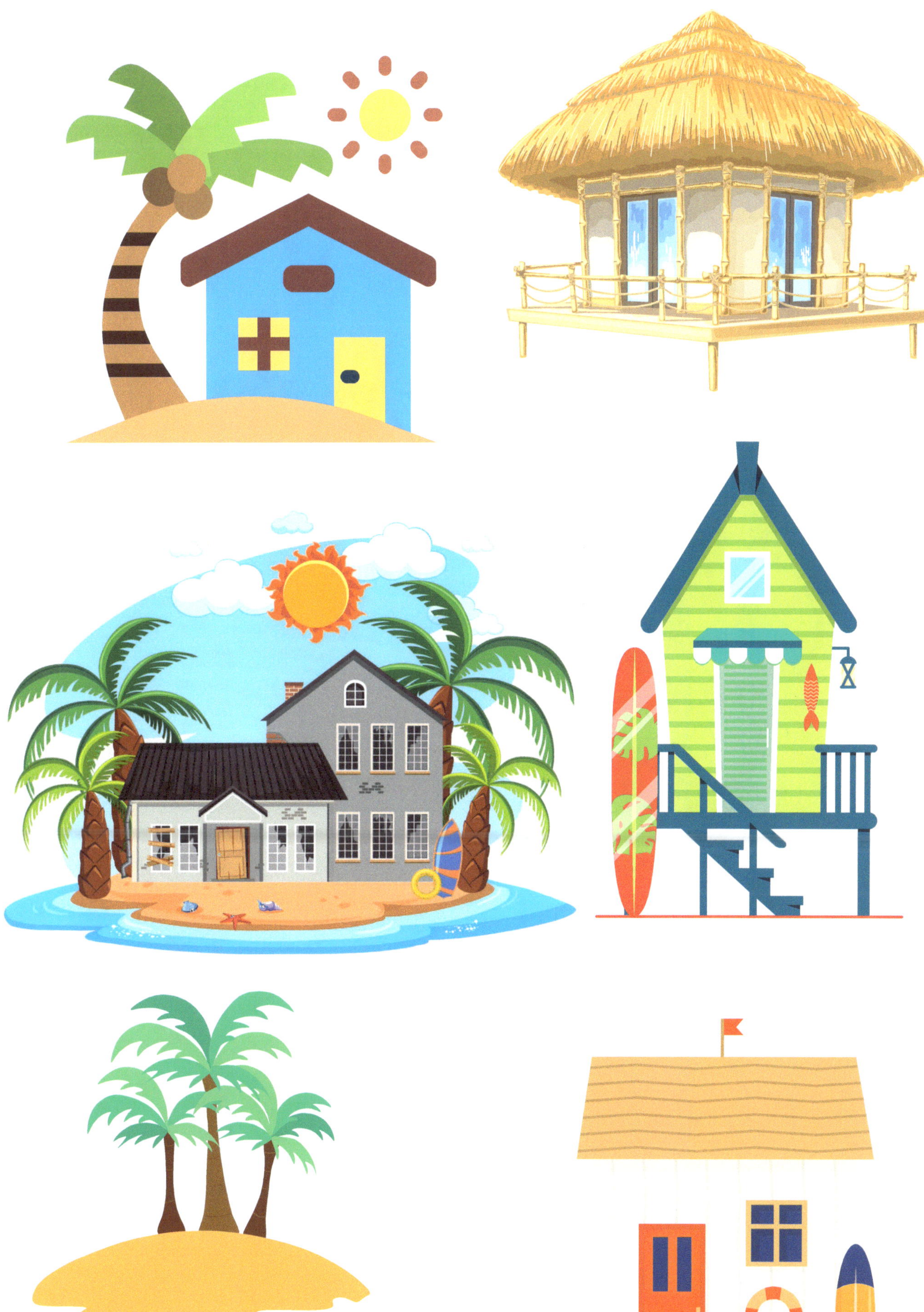

beach party

surf

fun

summer

sun AND sea

WOW!

POOL PARTY

Good vibes

Beach Please

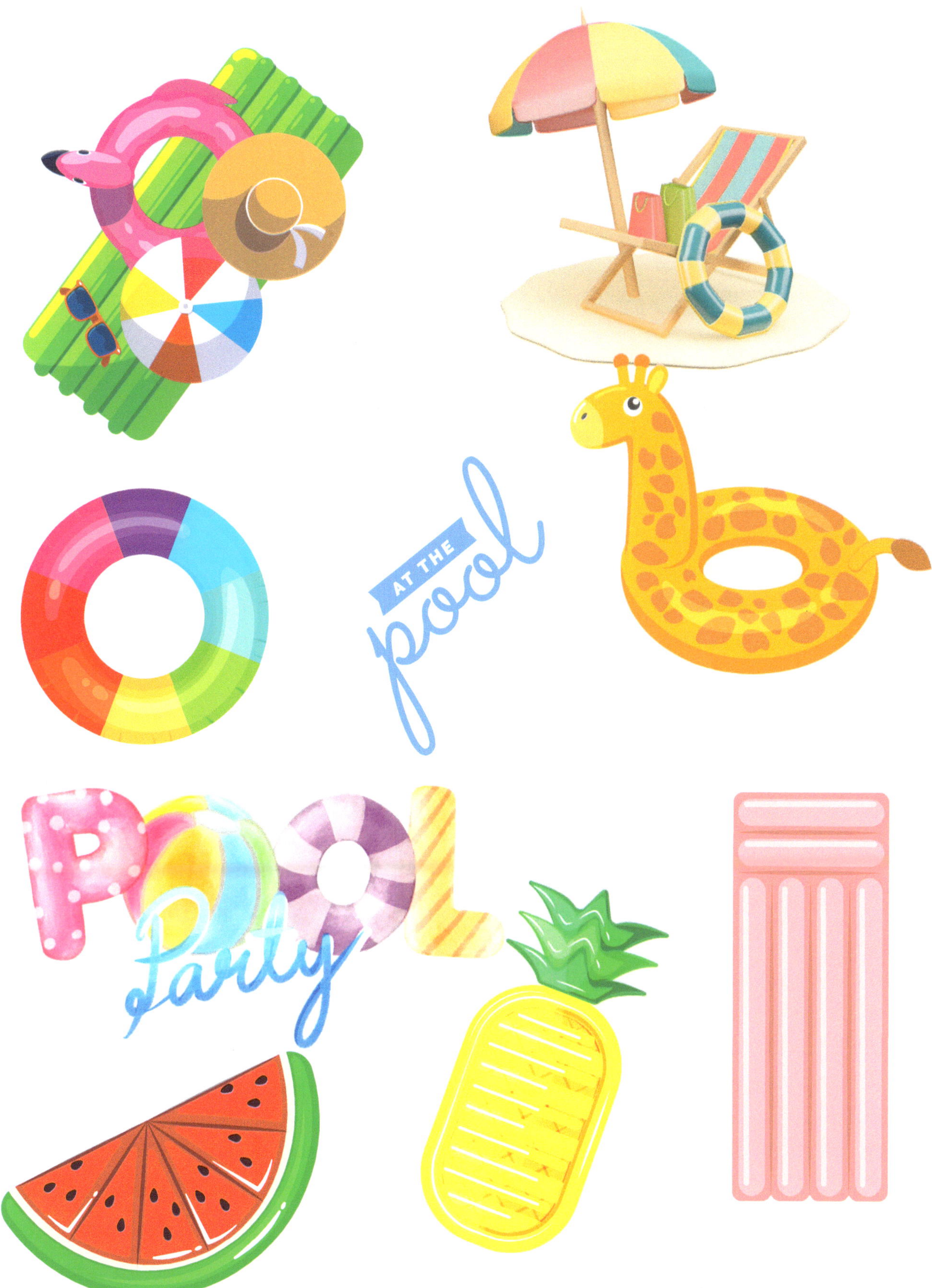

AT THE
pool
POOL
Party

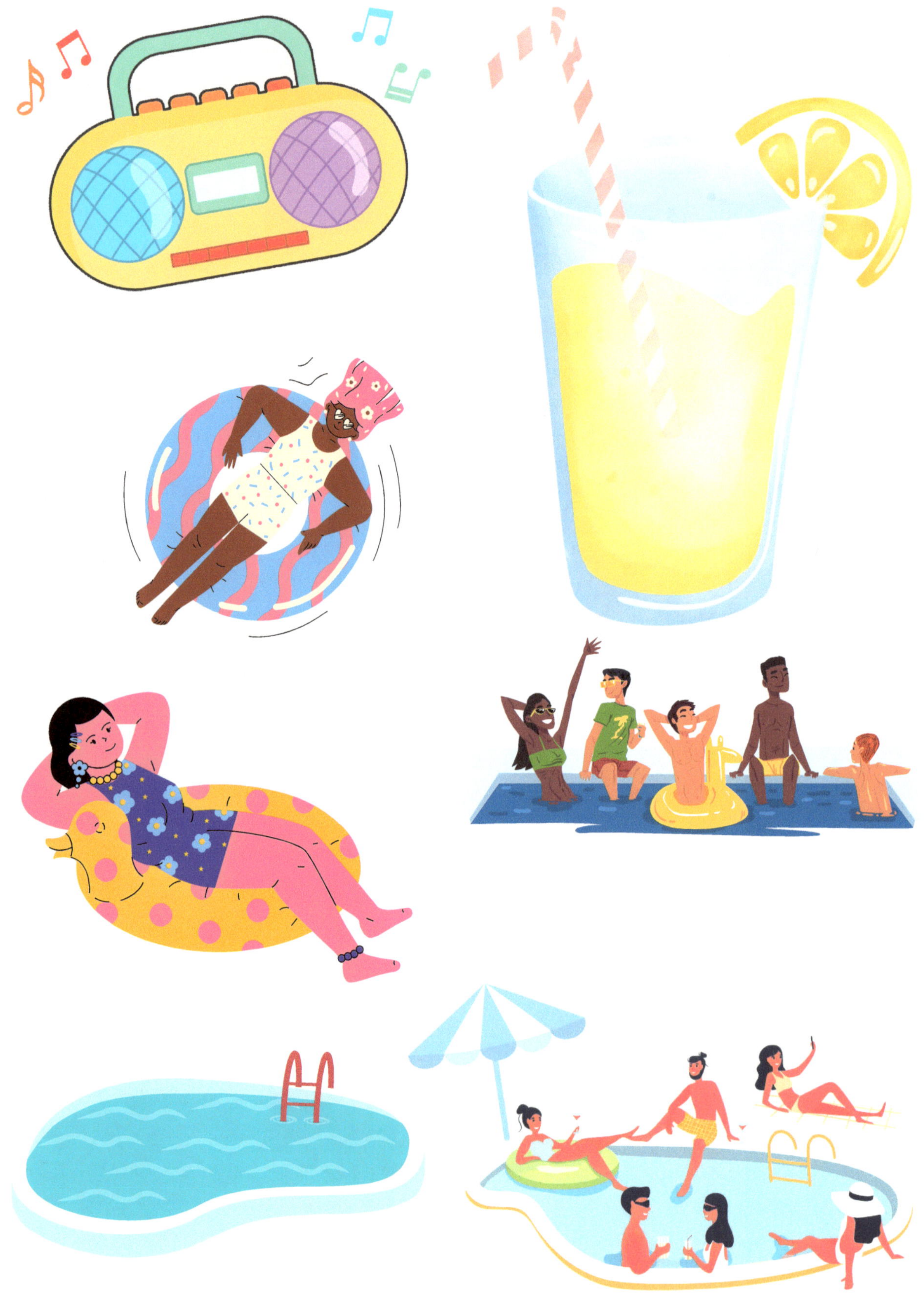

Fruits

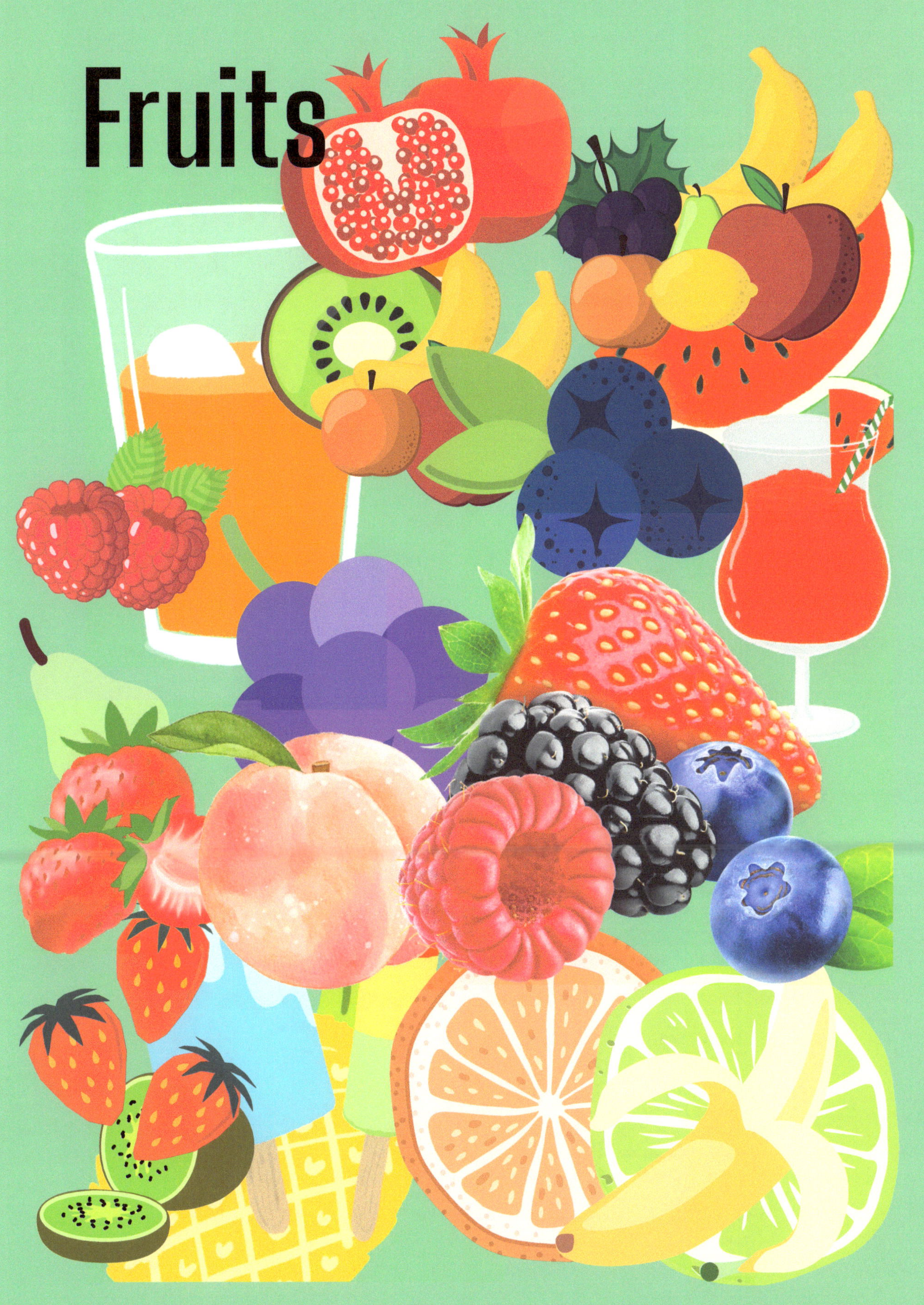

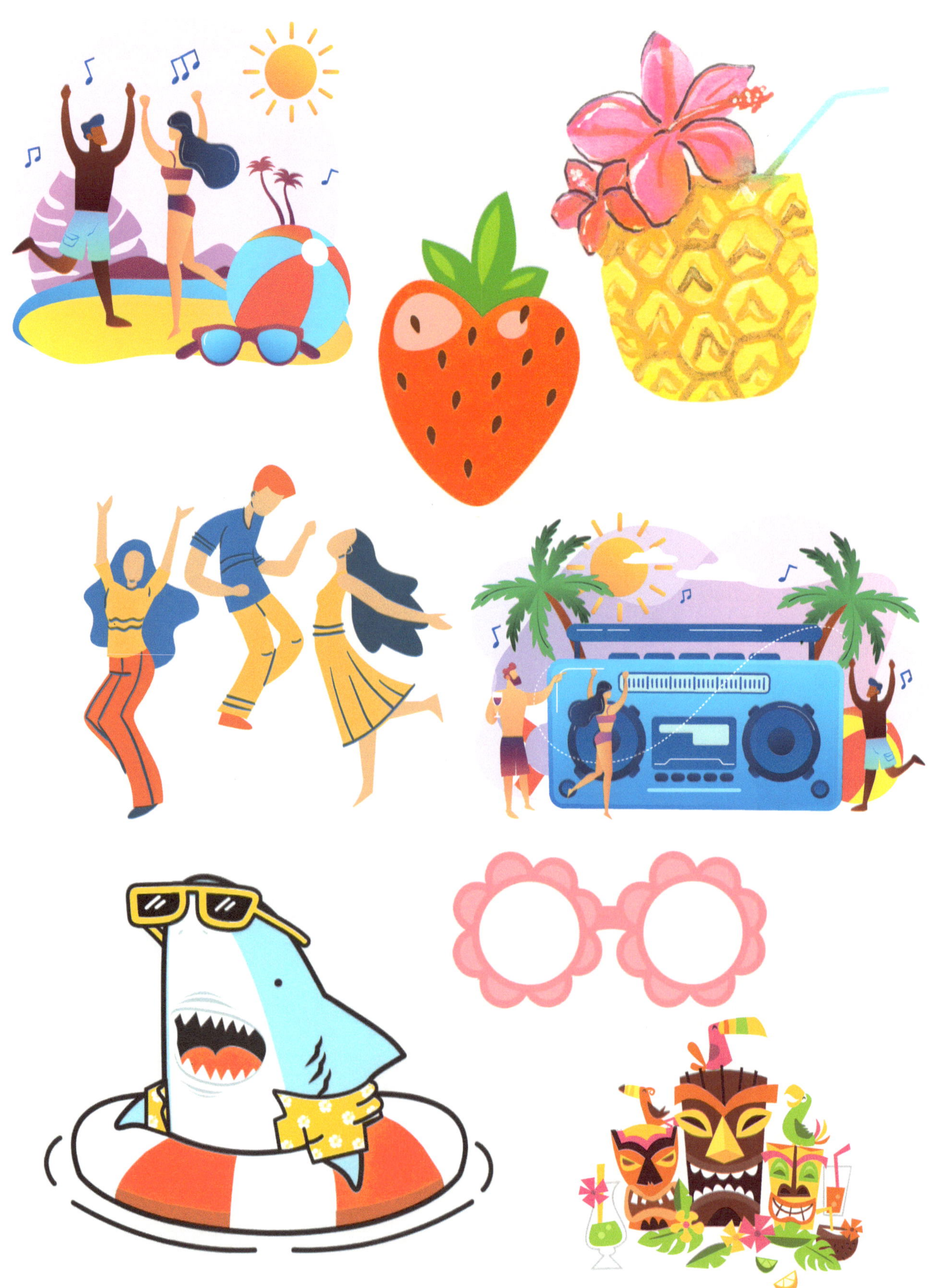

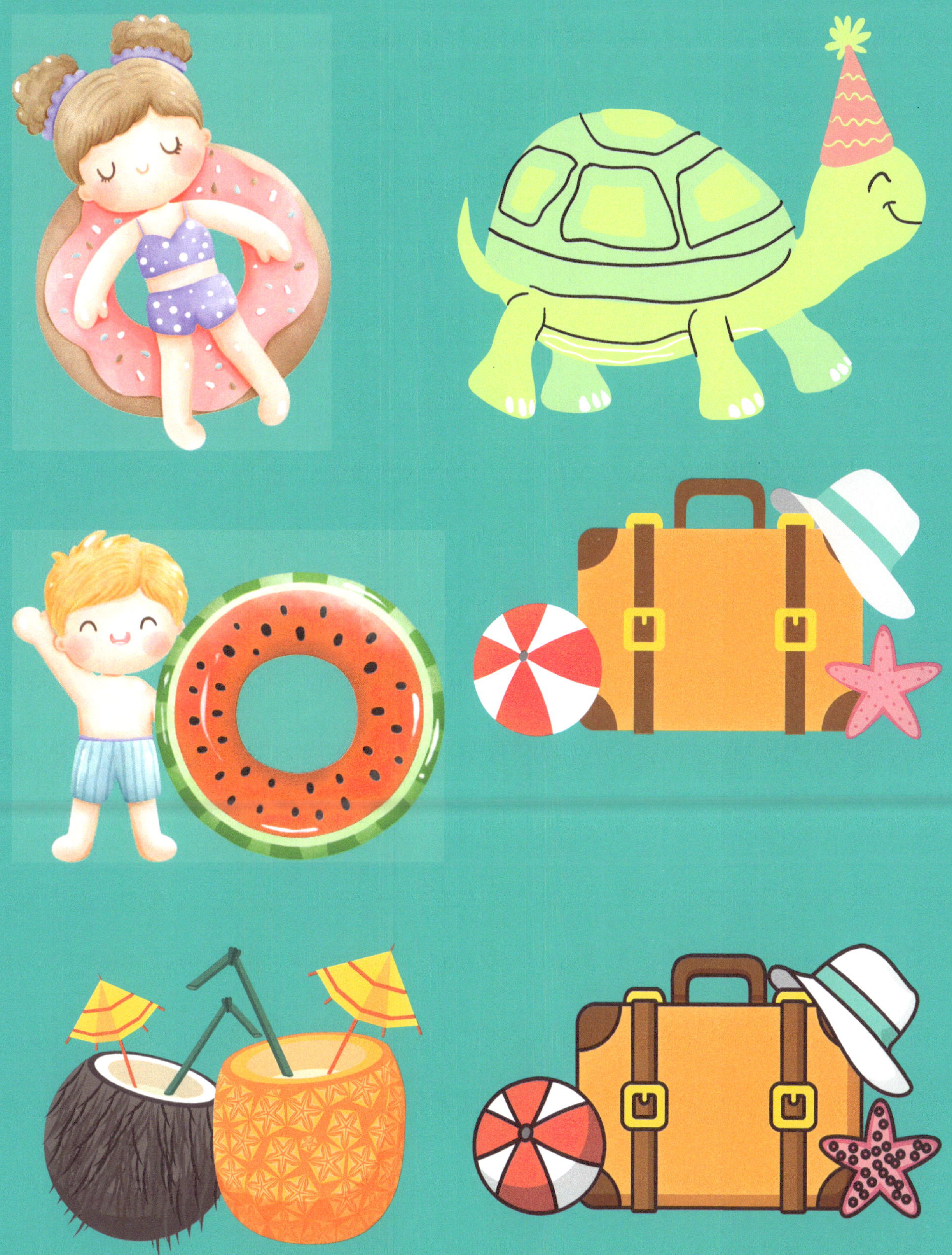

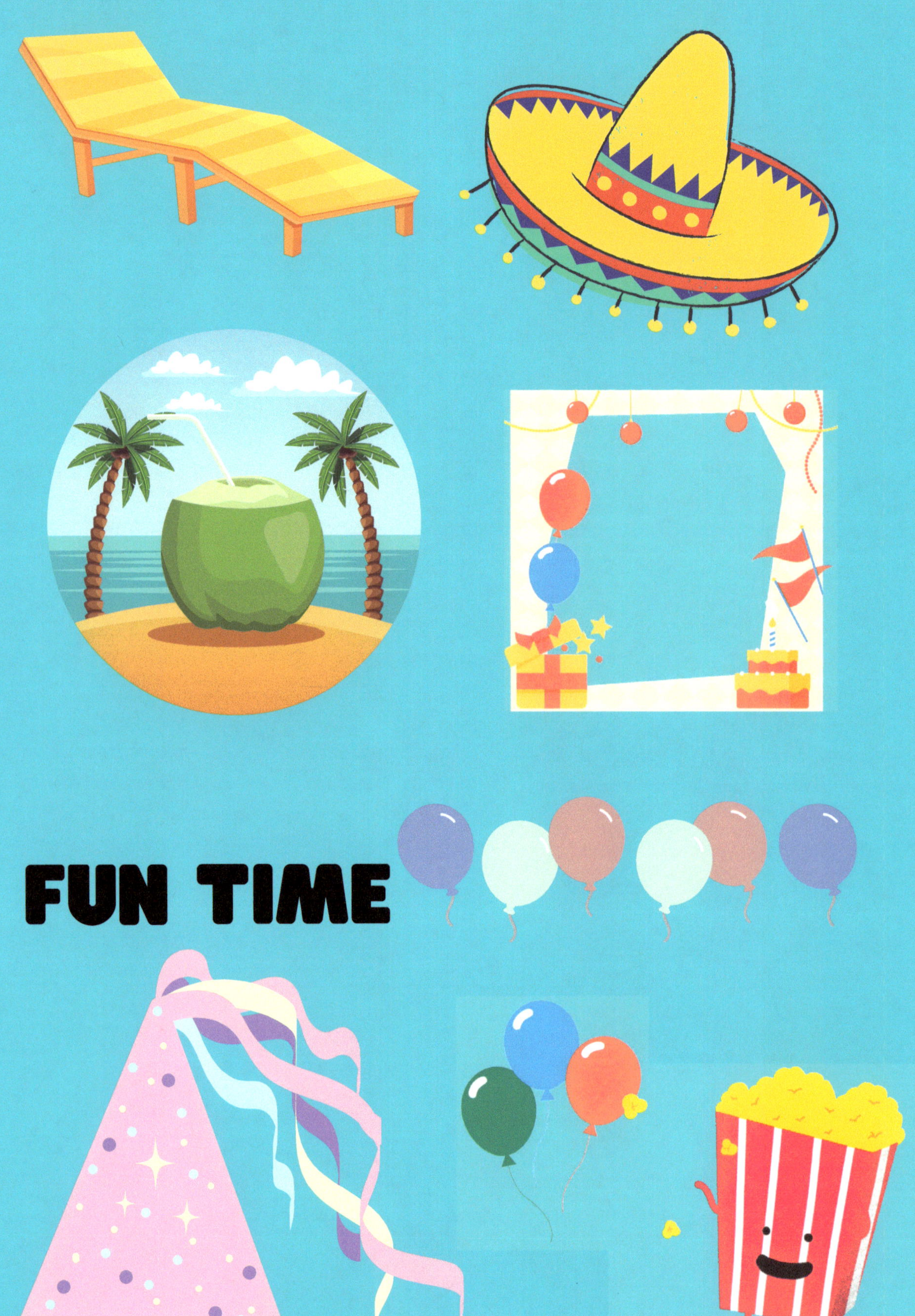
FUN TIME

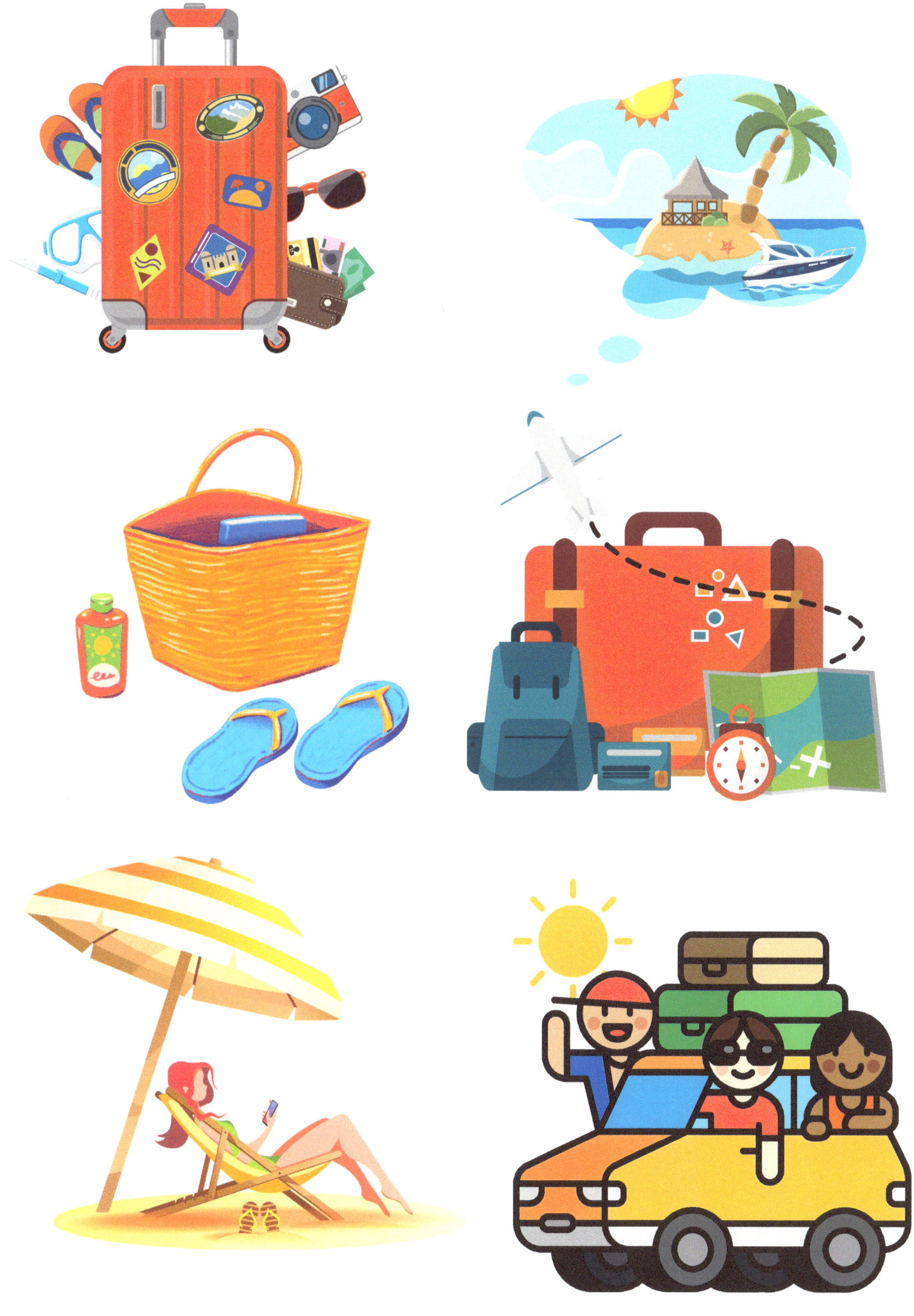

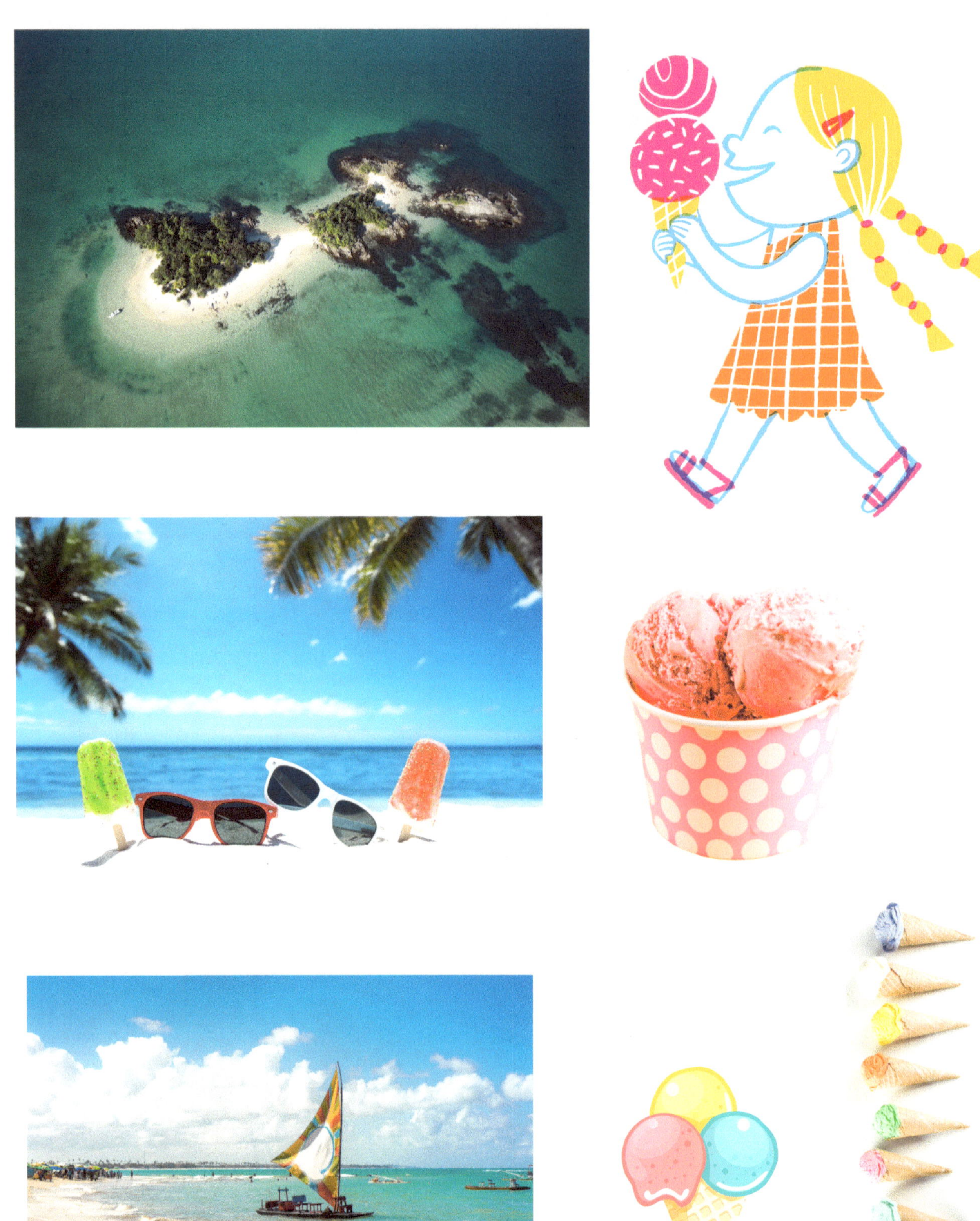

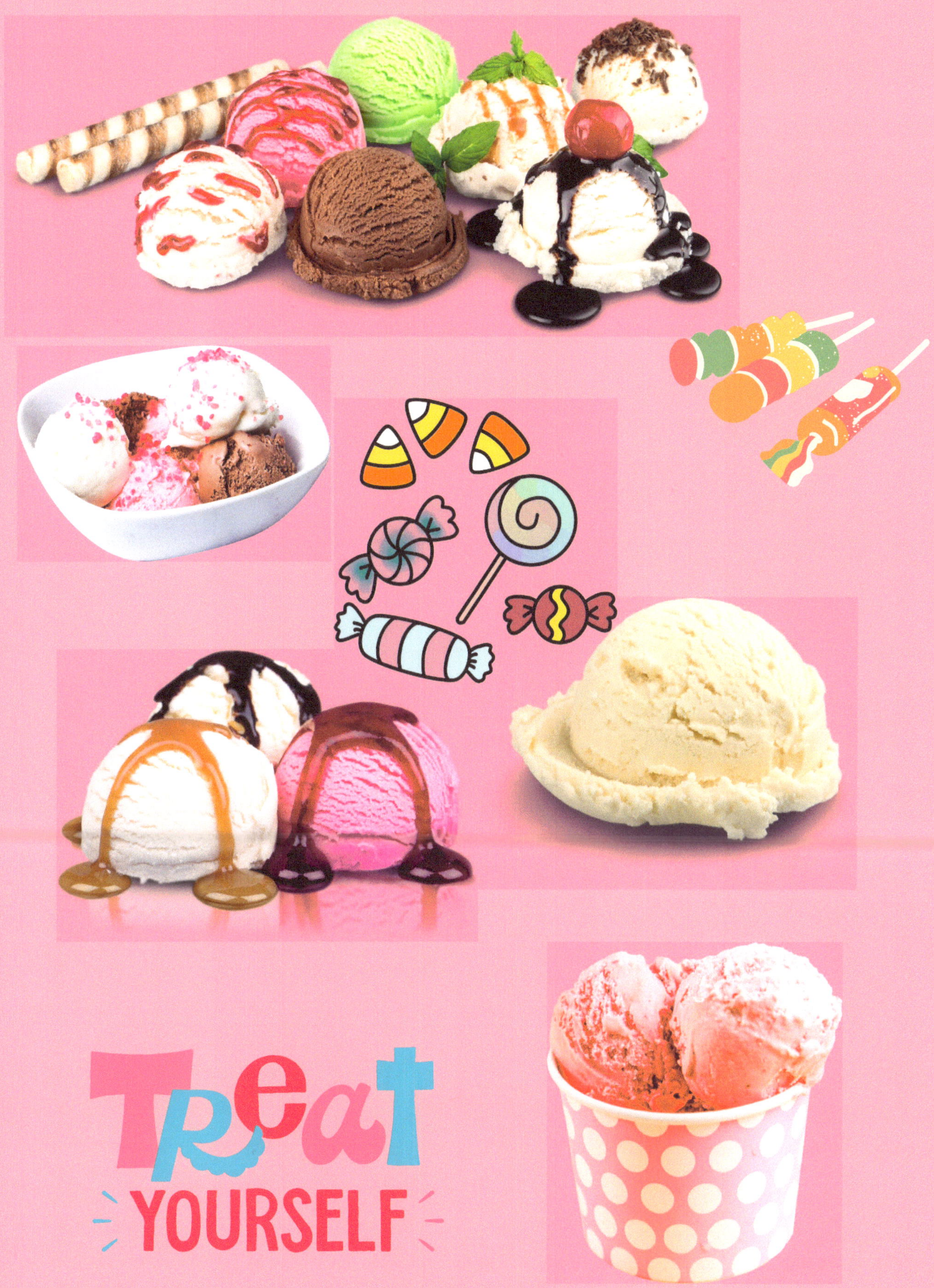

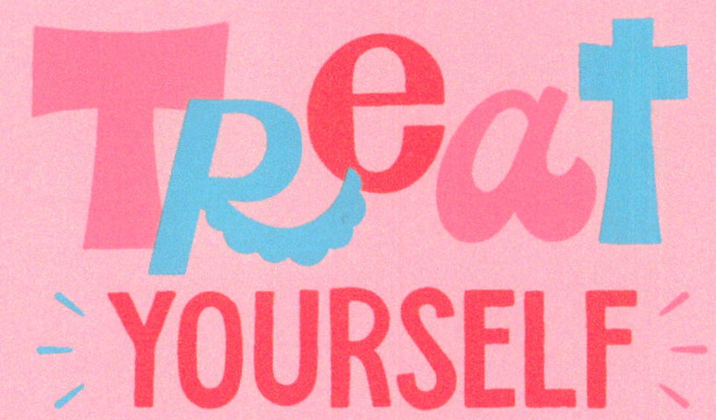
TReat
YOURSELF
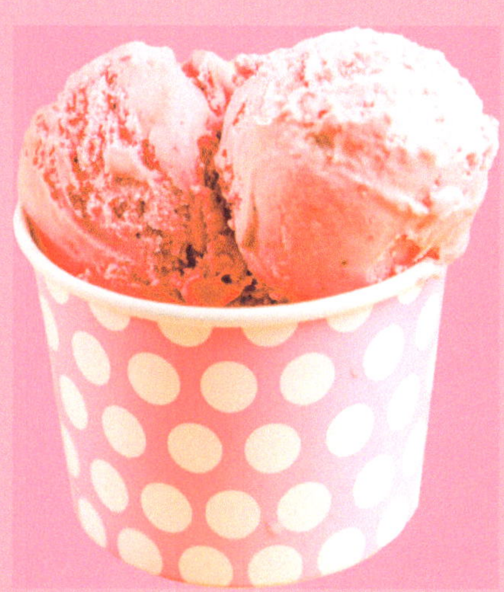

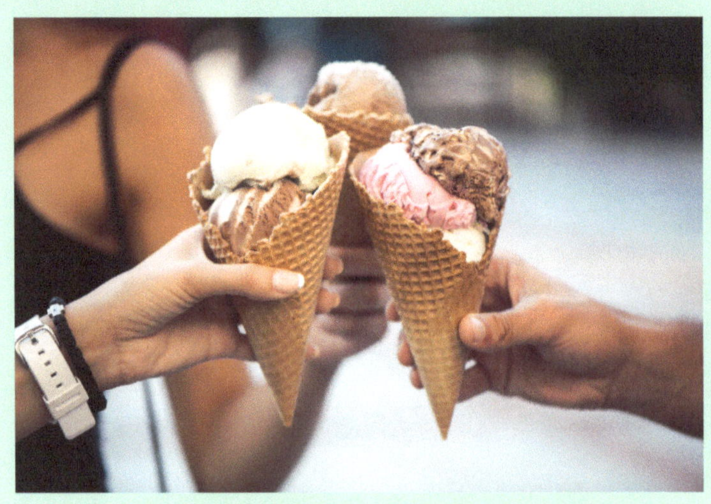
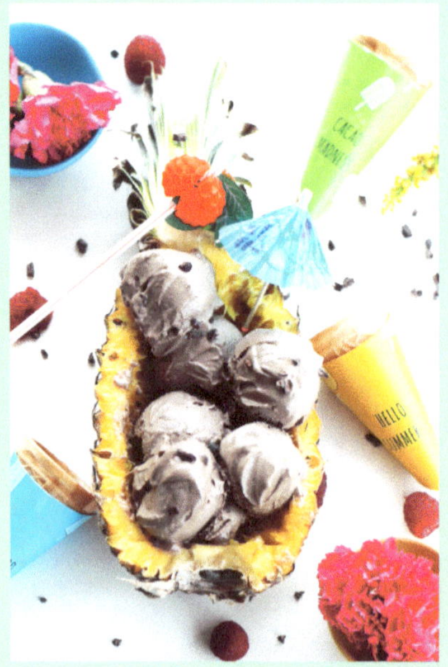
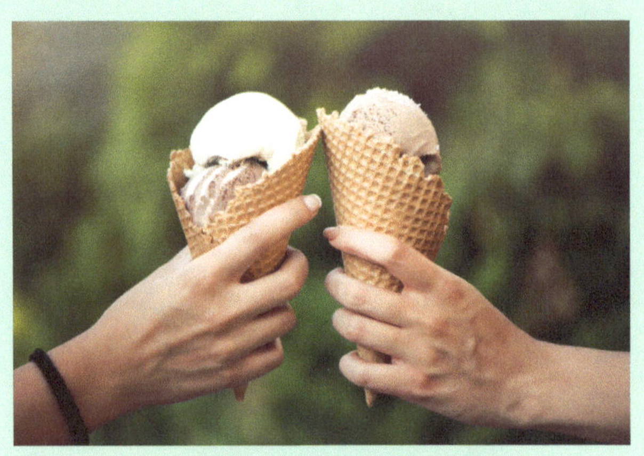
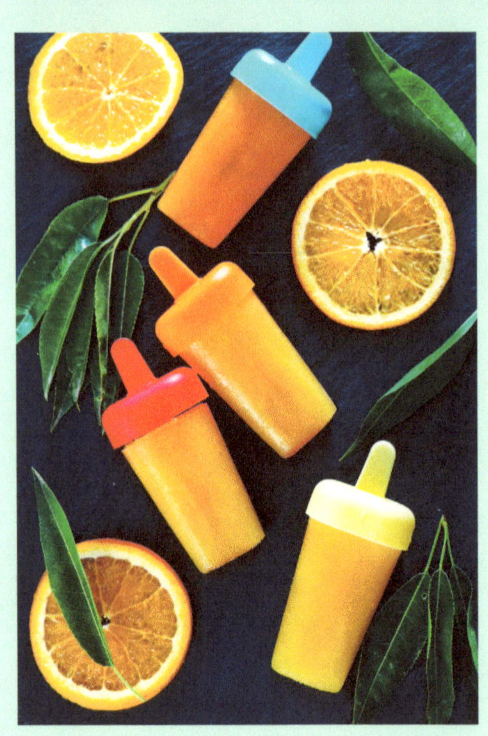
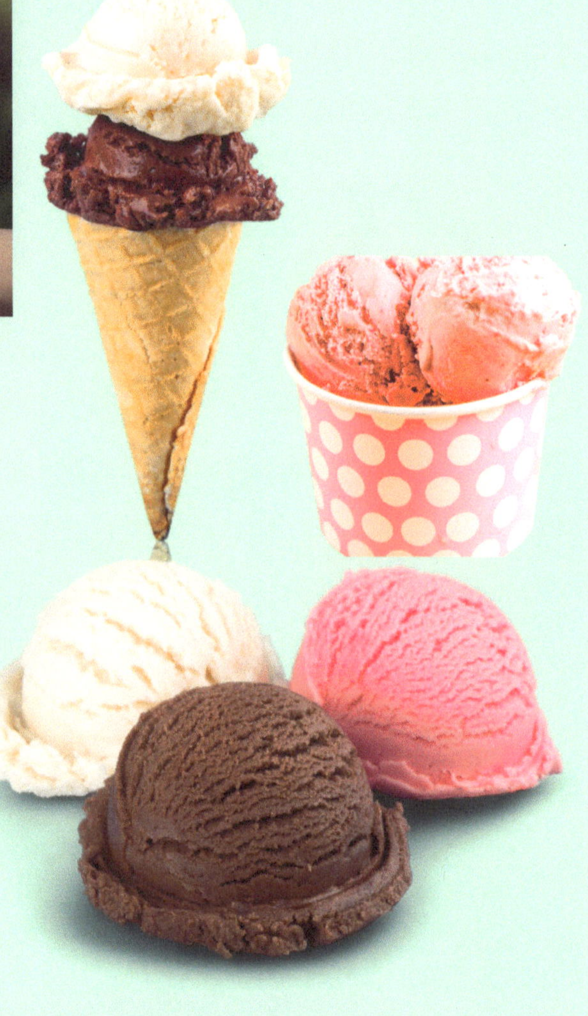

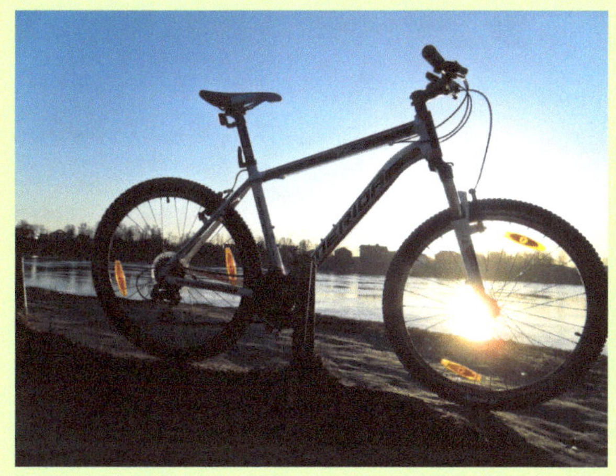
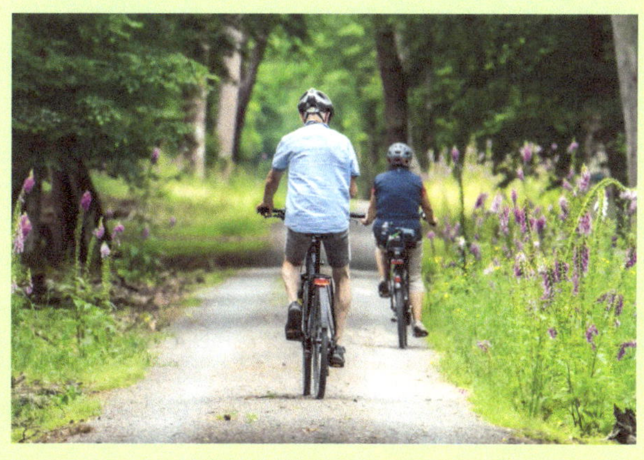
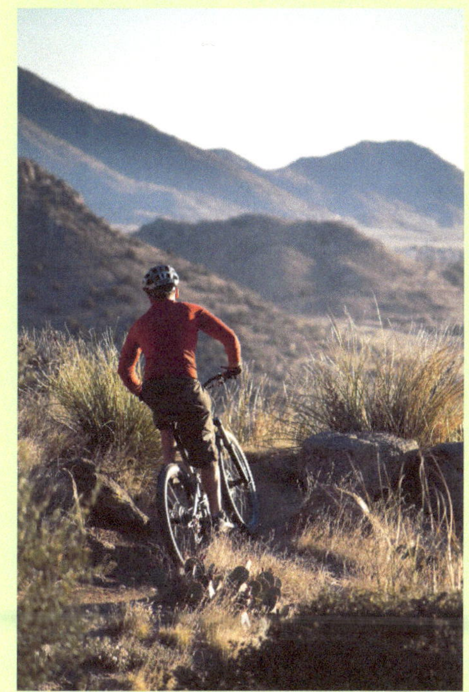
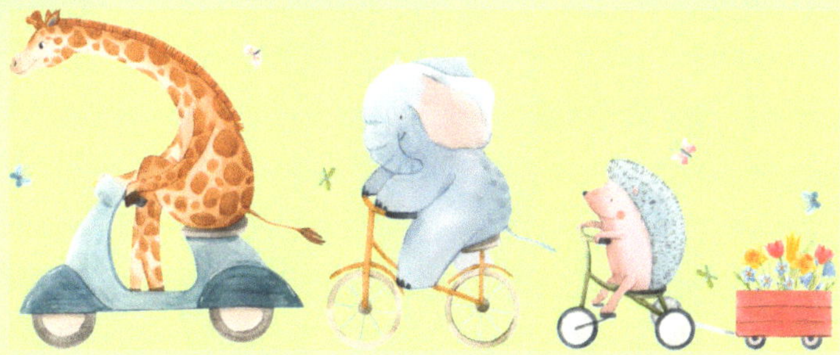
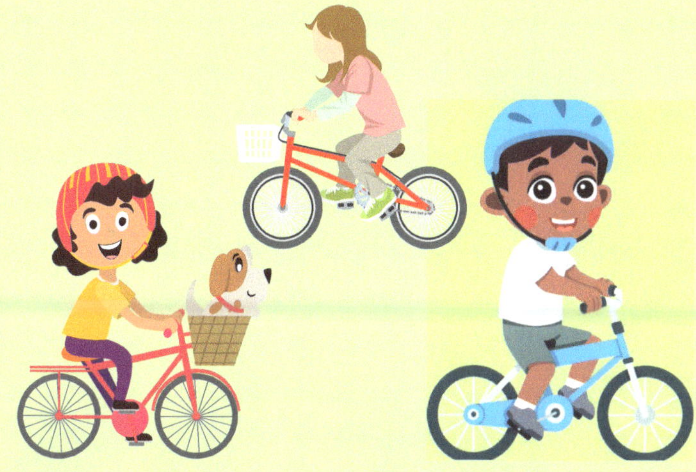
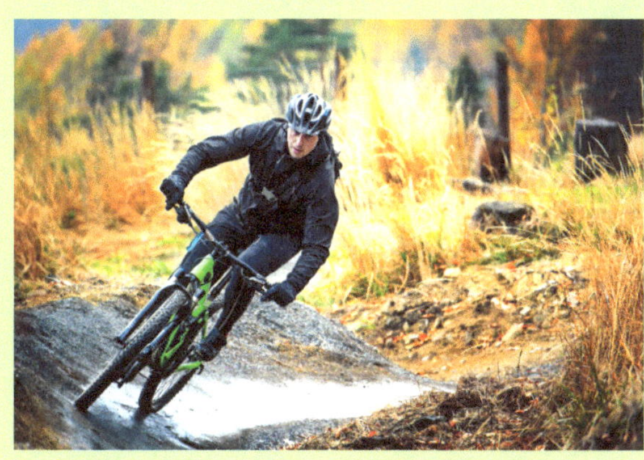
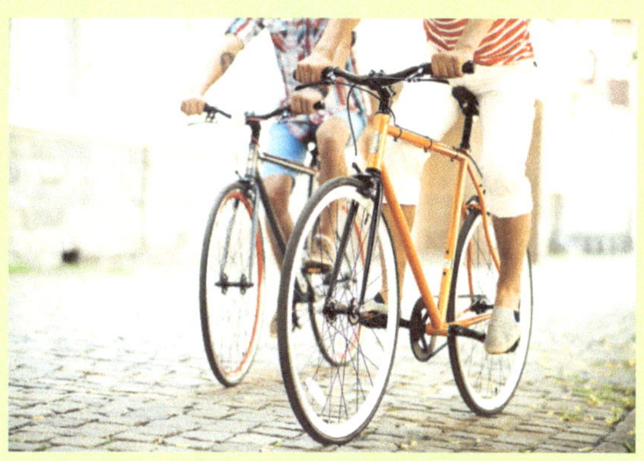

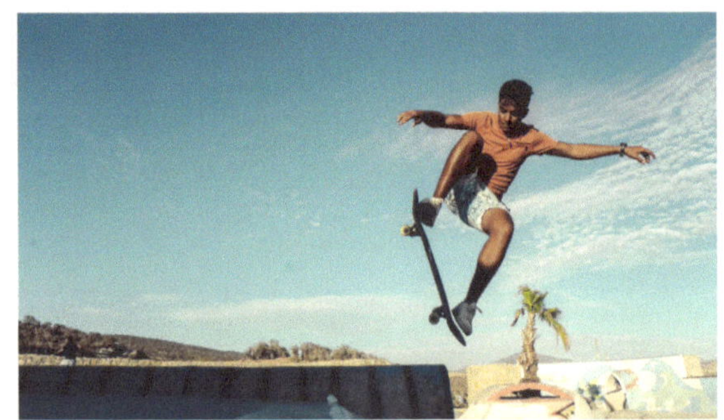

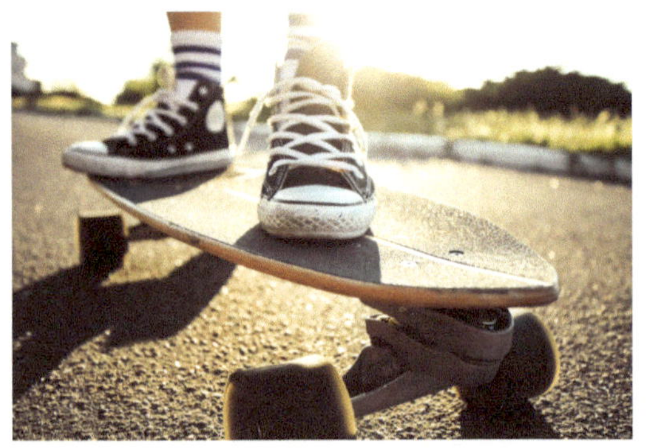

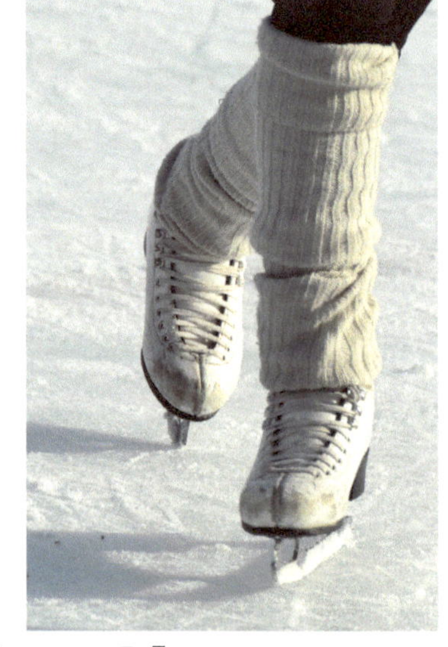

fun

Roller Skating

SKATEBOARD

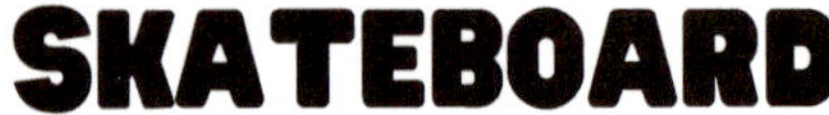

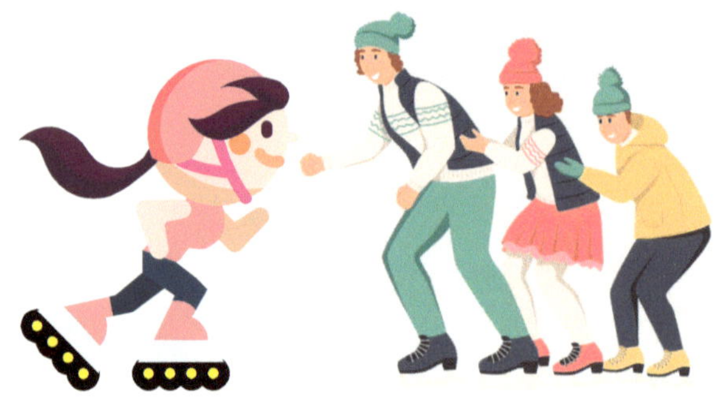

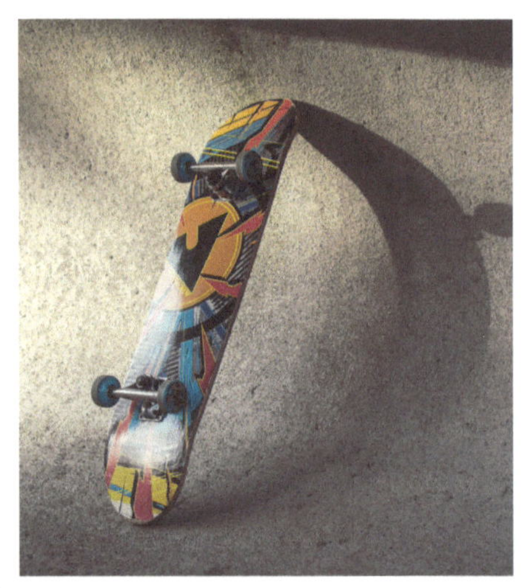

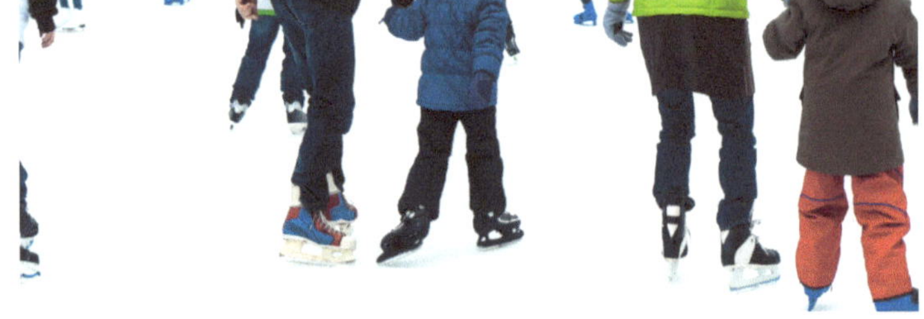

ICE SKATE

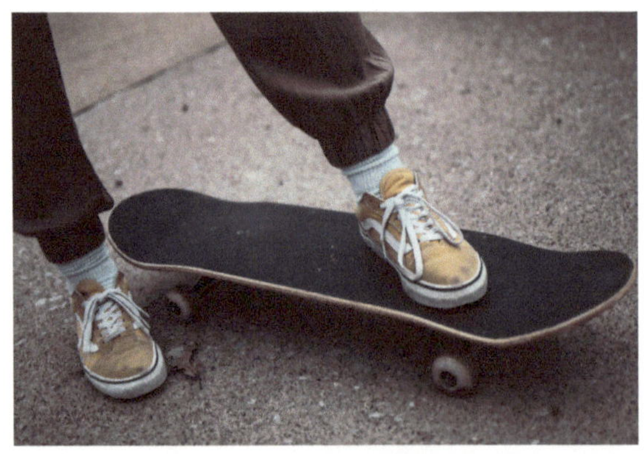

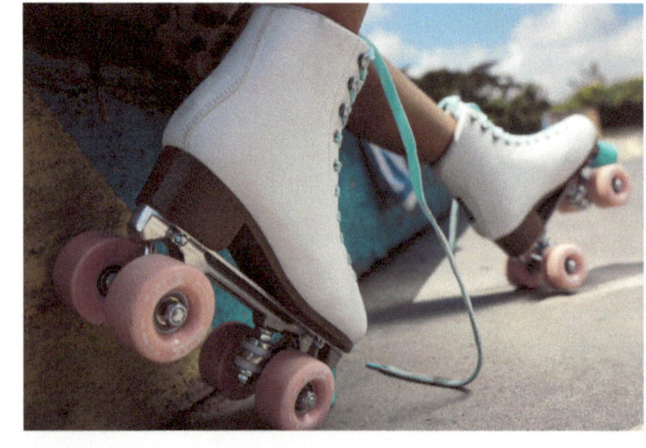

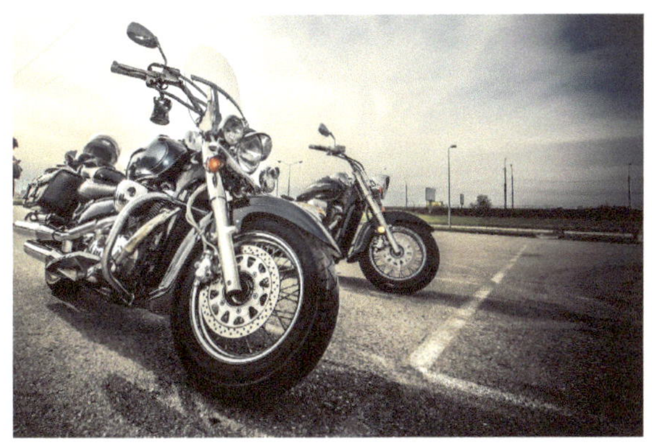
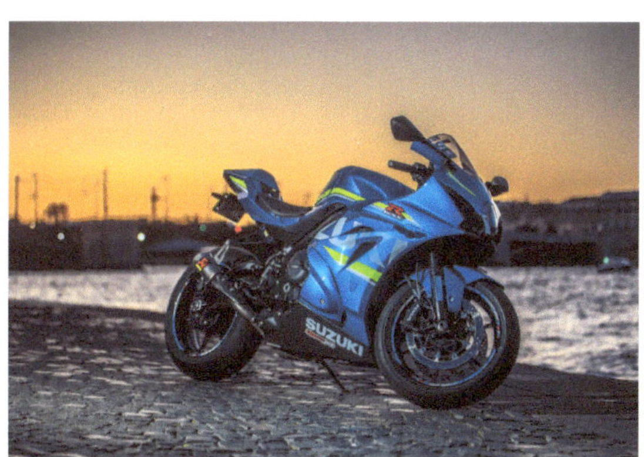
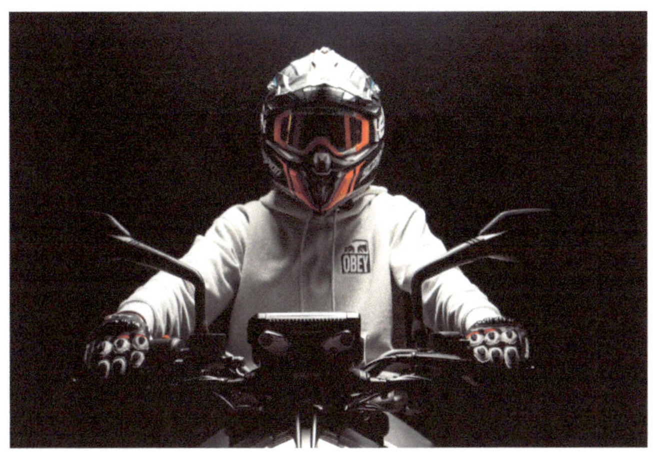
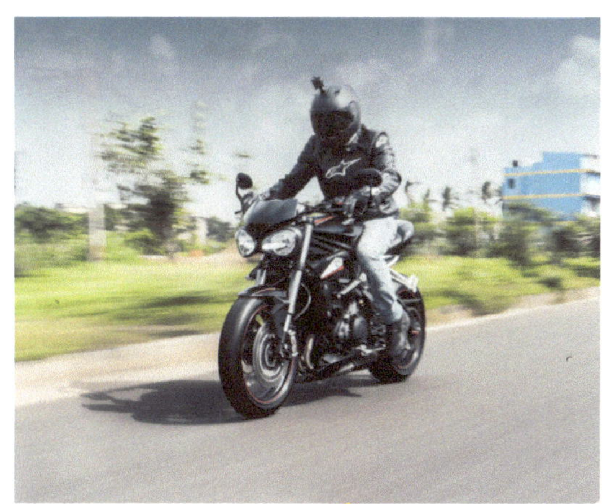

fun

WOW!

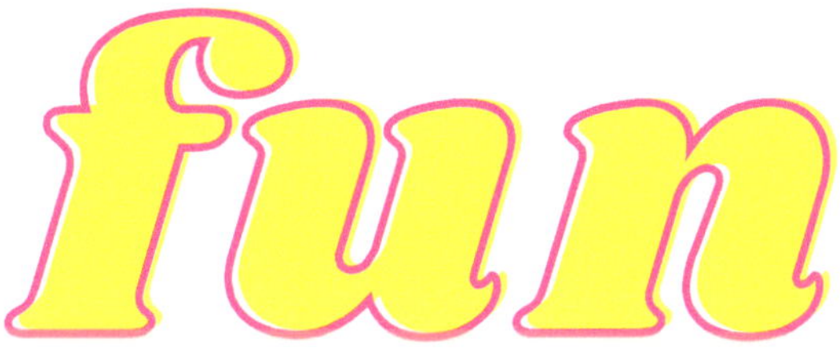
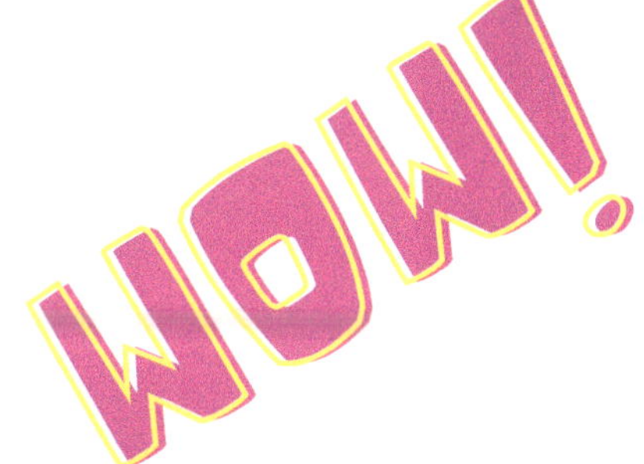
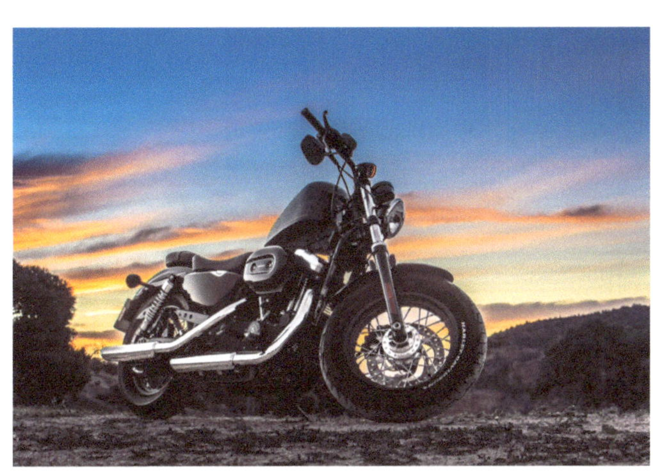
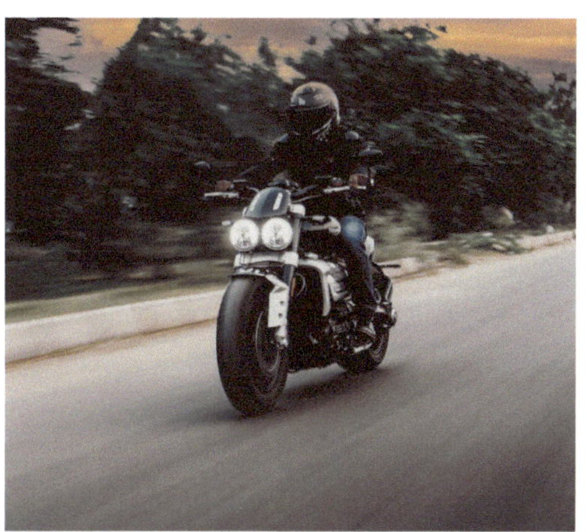

CYCLES
BIKES

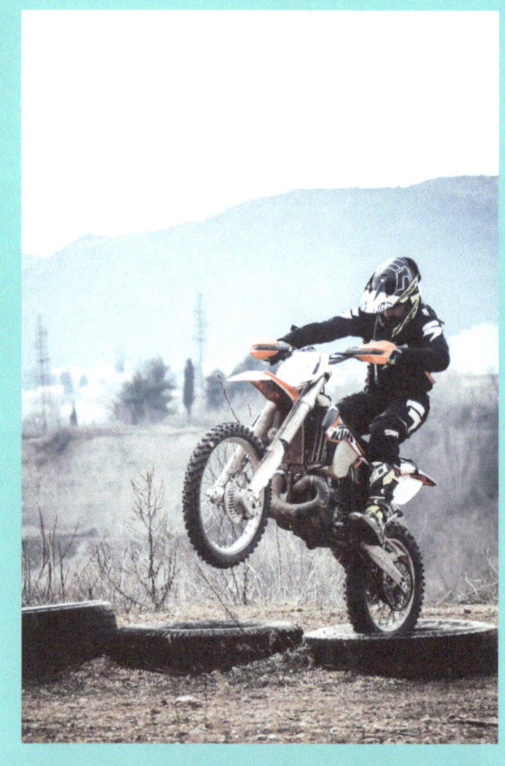

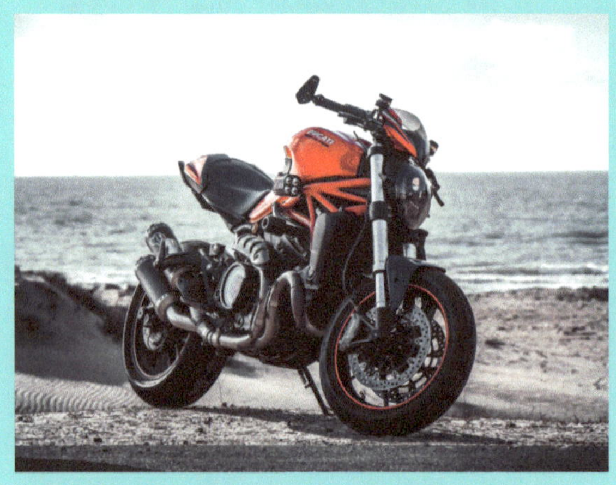

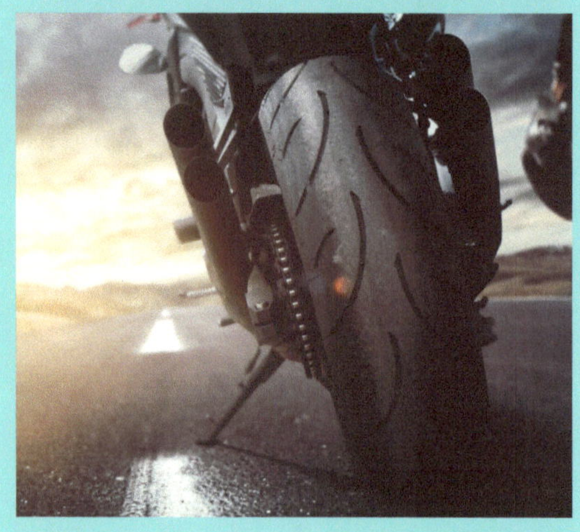

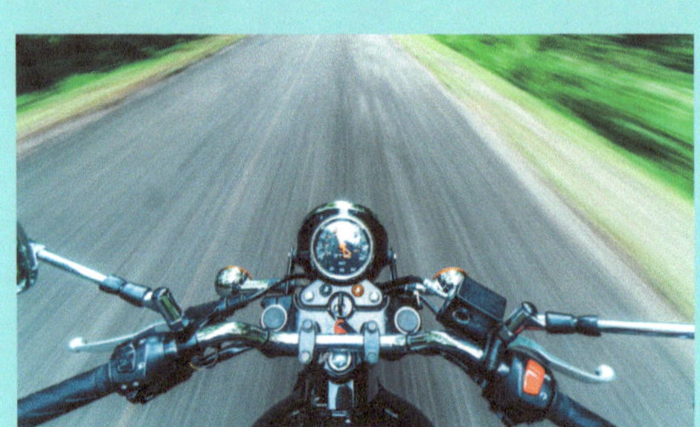

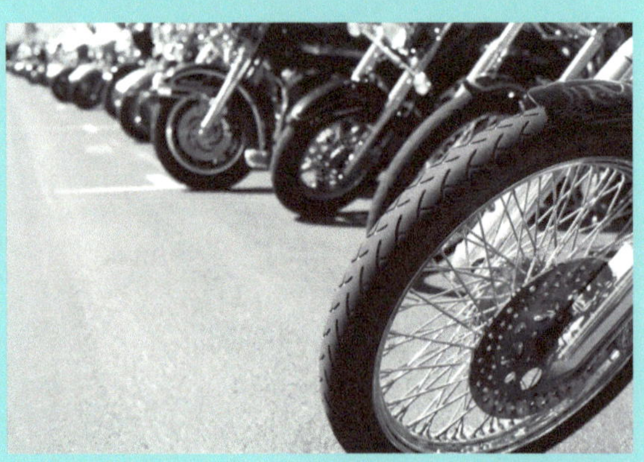

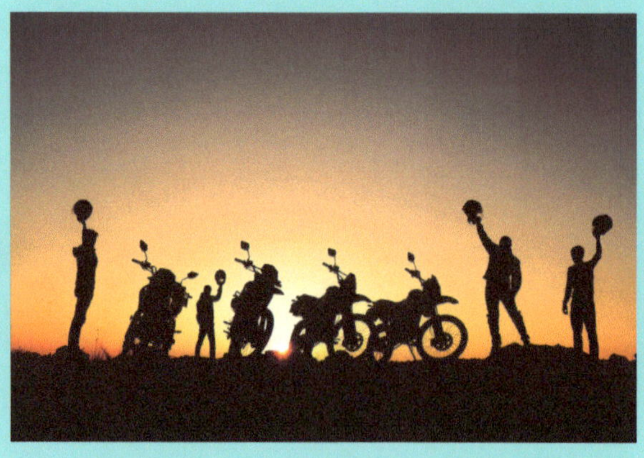

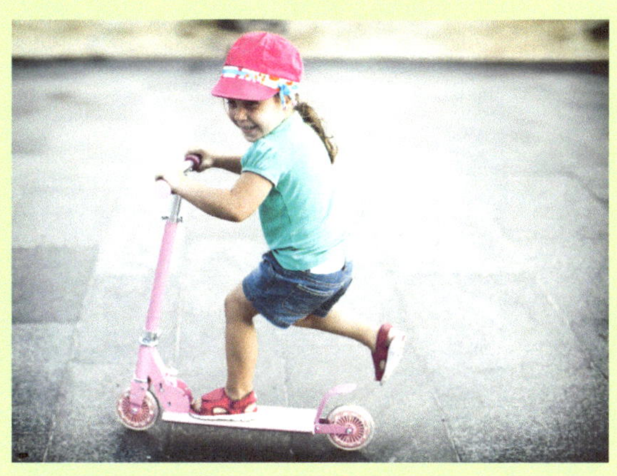

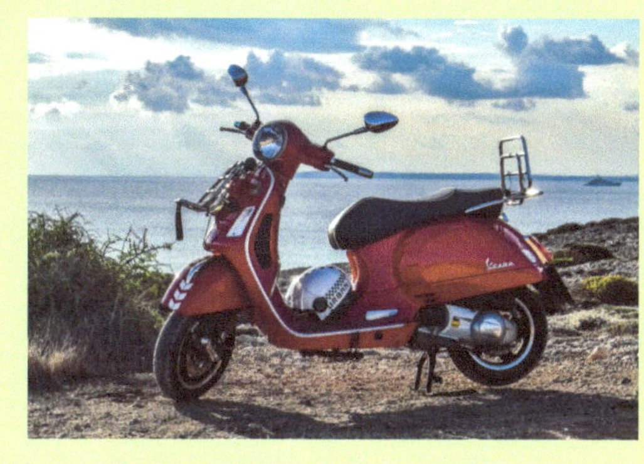

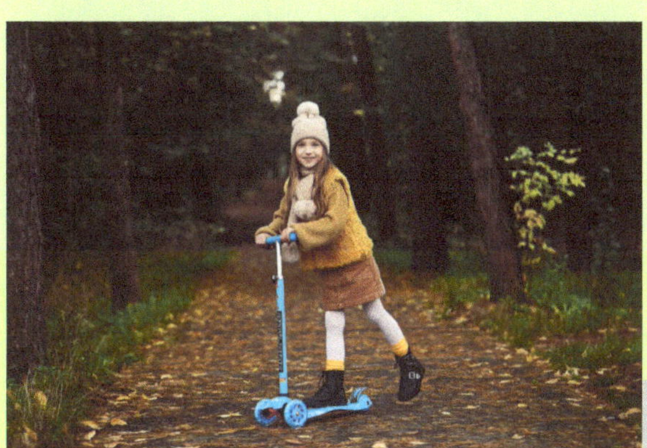

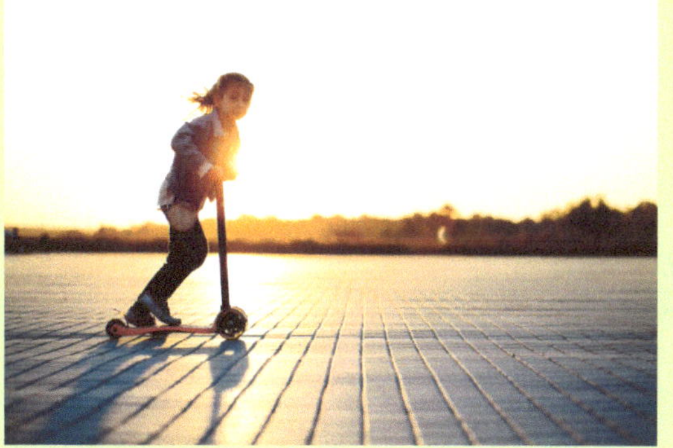

GLOW

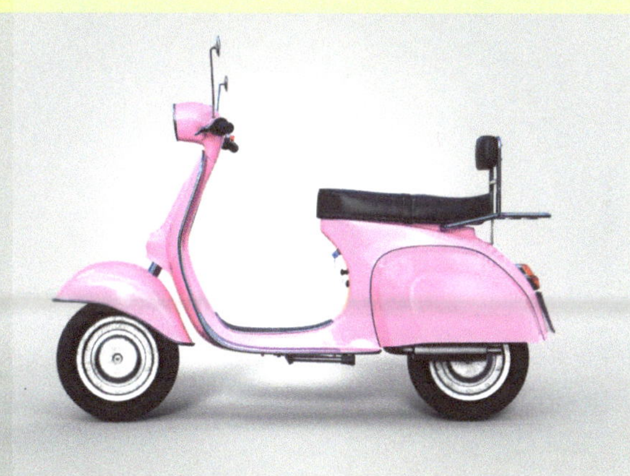

SCOOTER FUN

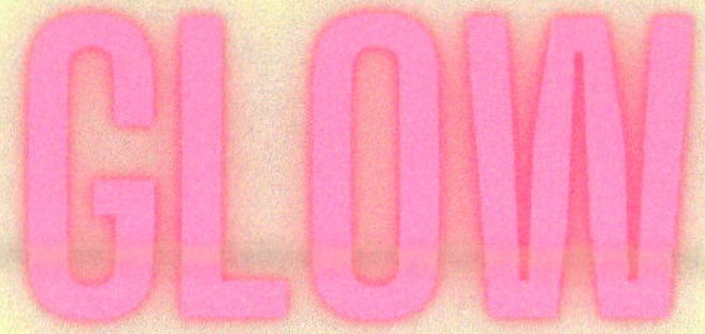

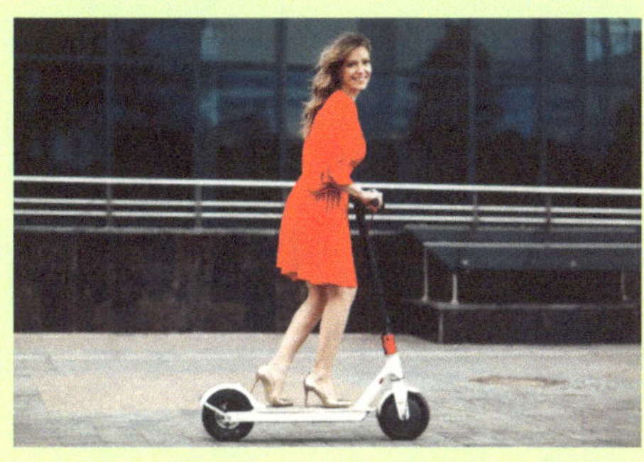

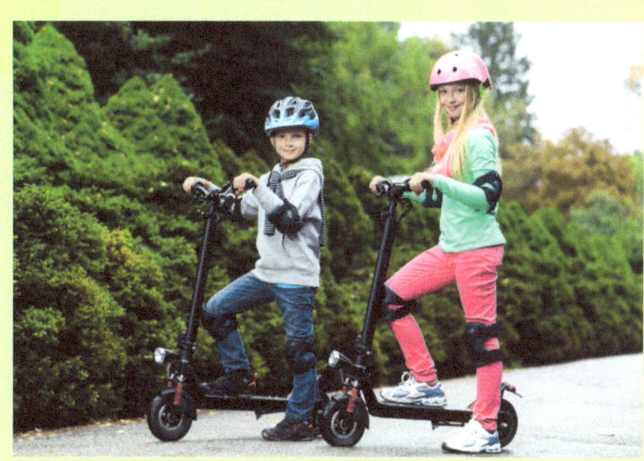

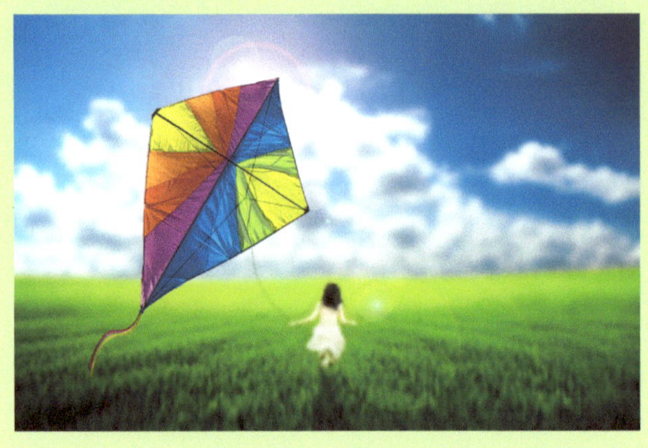
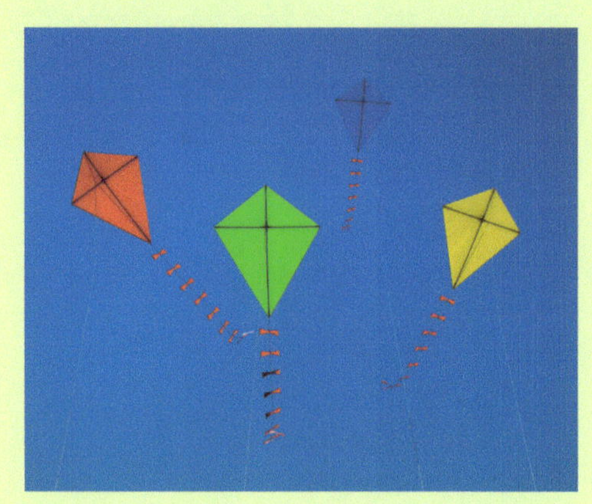

KITE FUN

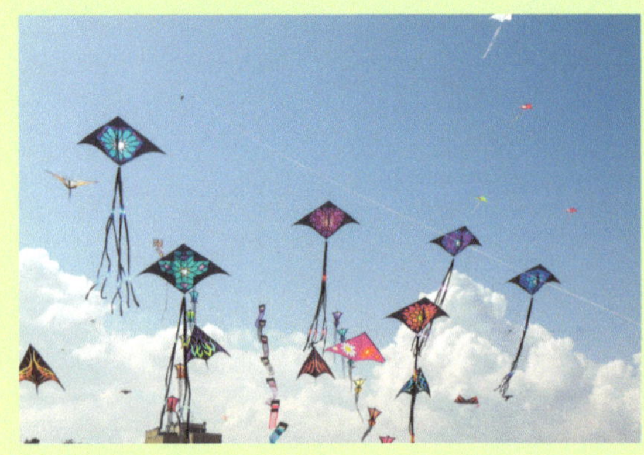
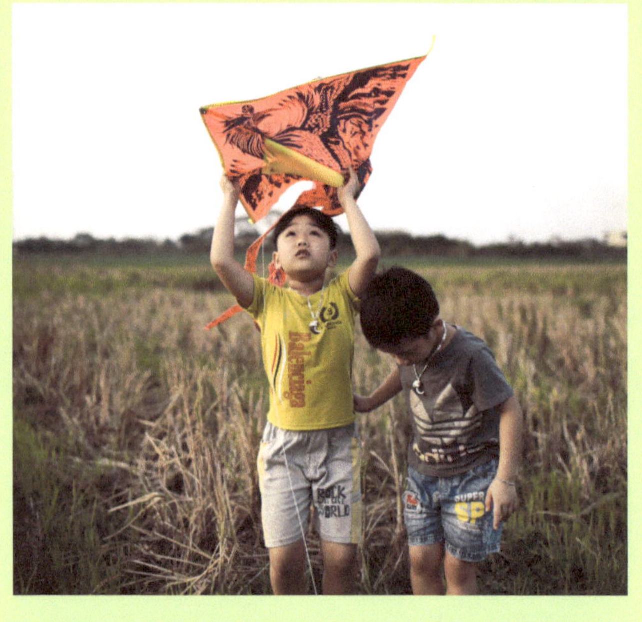
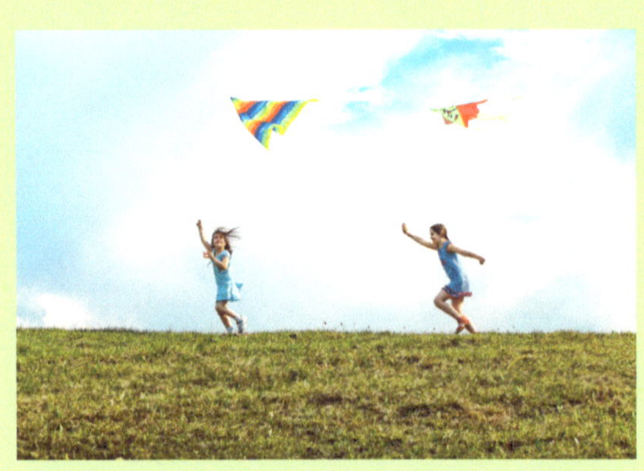
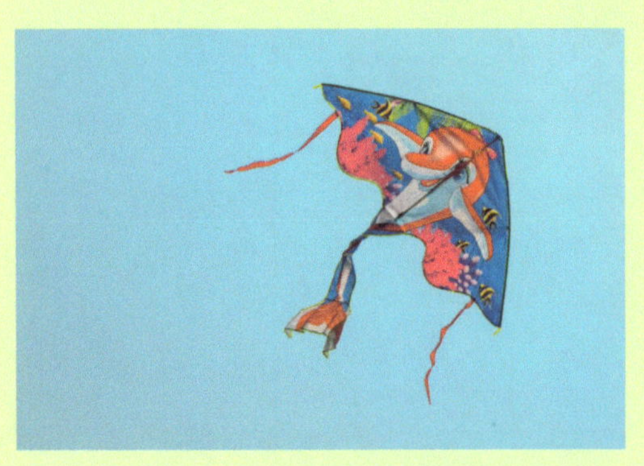
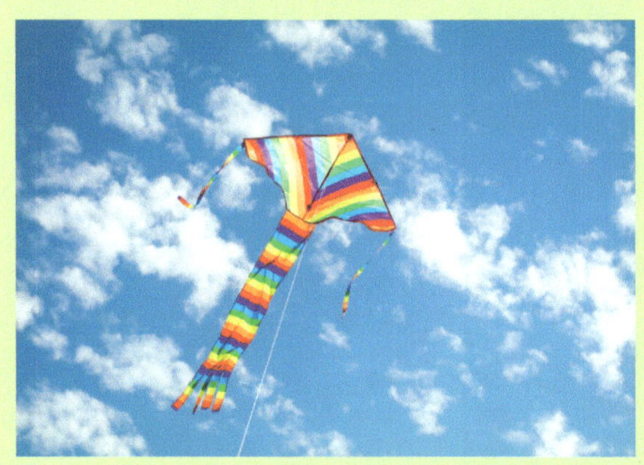

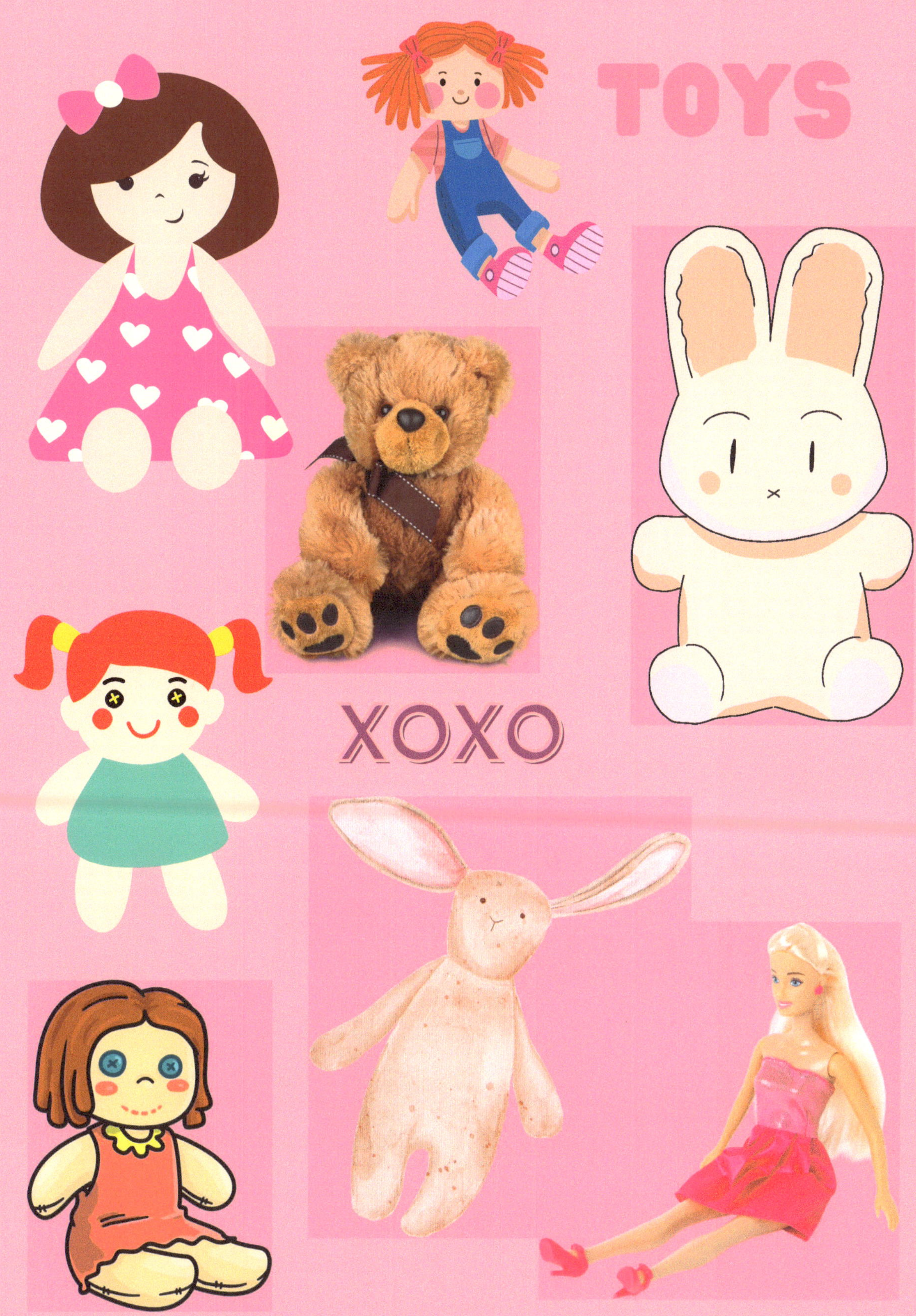

TOYS
XOXO

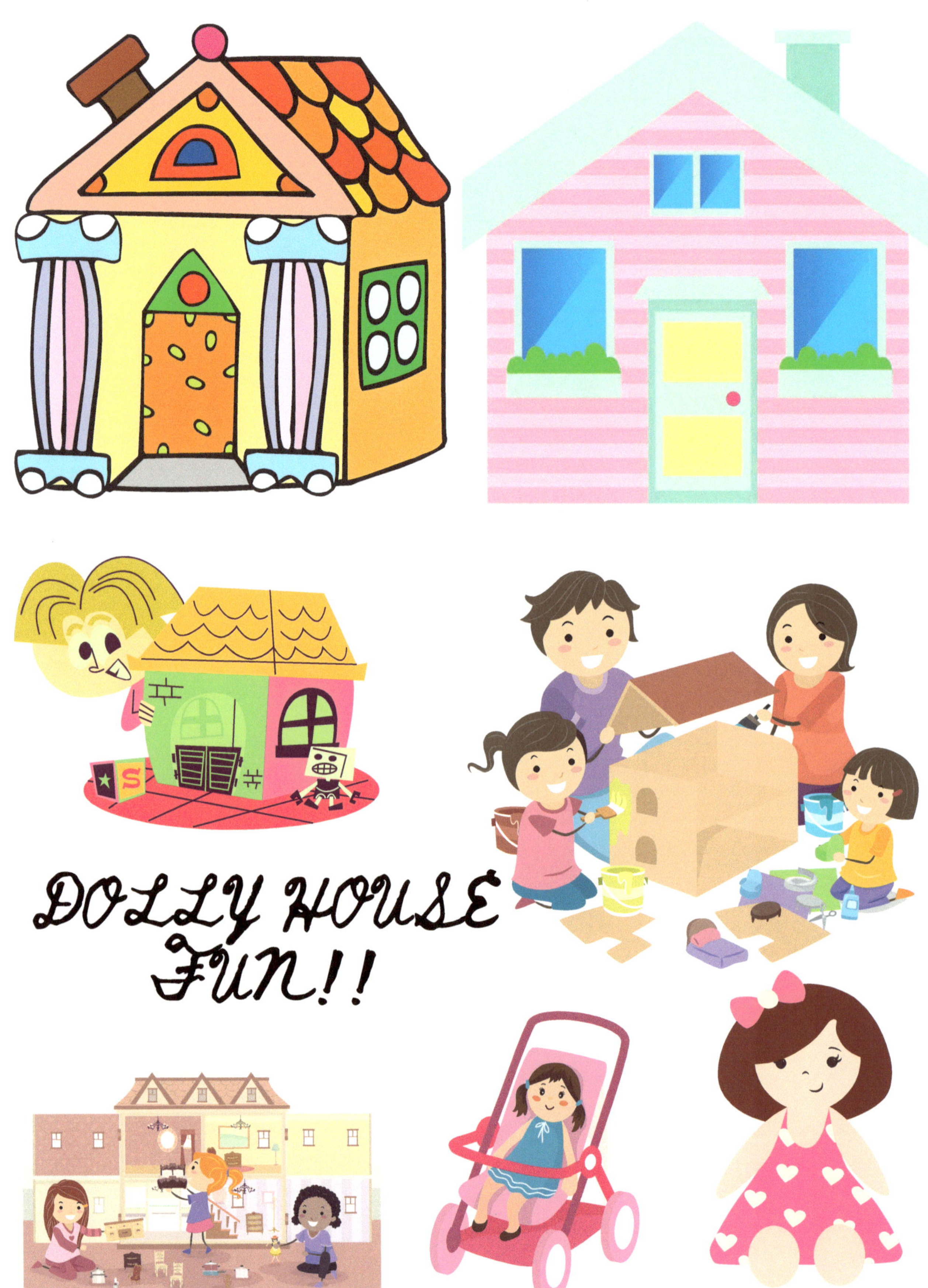
DOLLY HOUSE
FUN!!

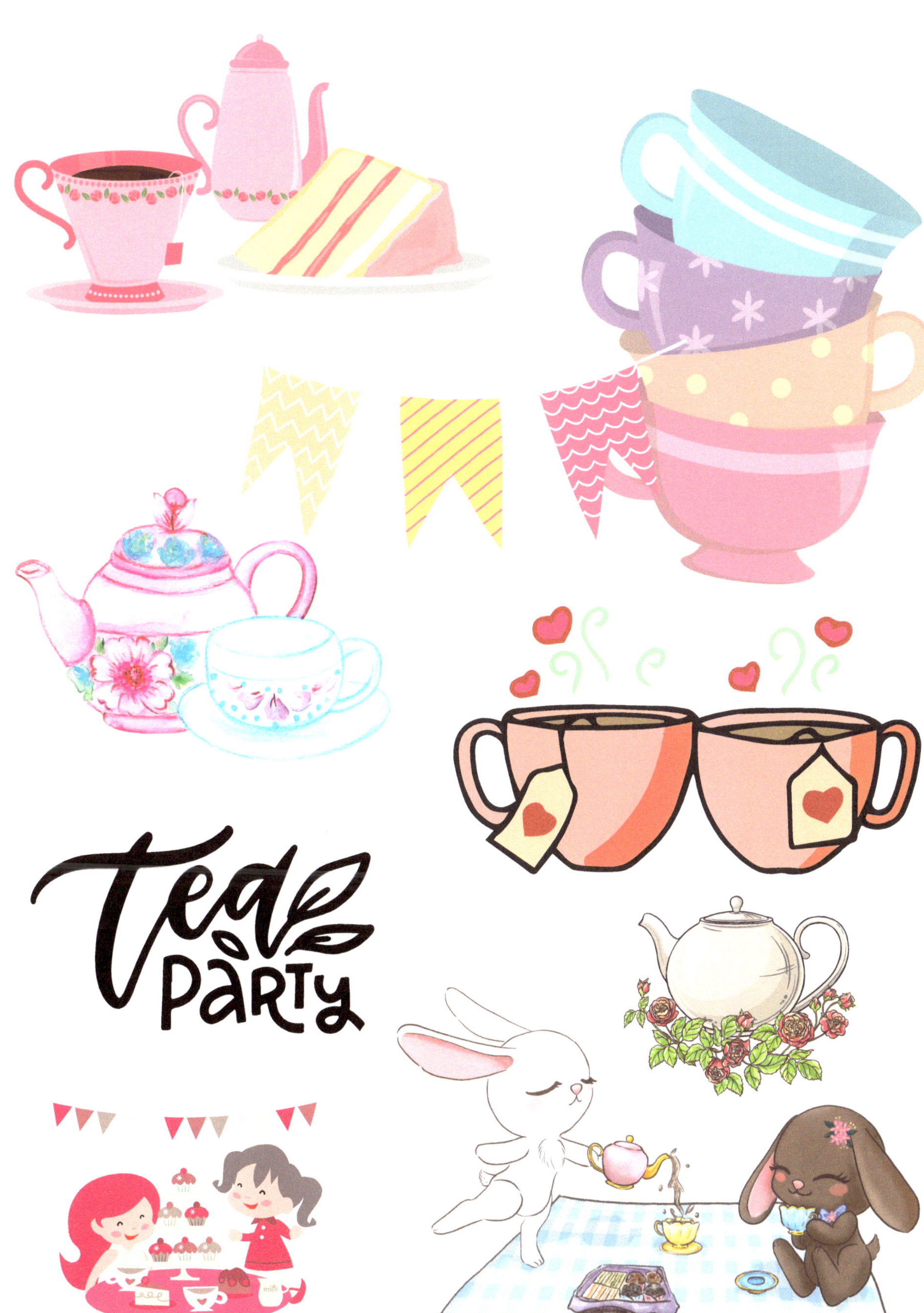

Tea
Party

TEA PARTY FUN

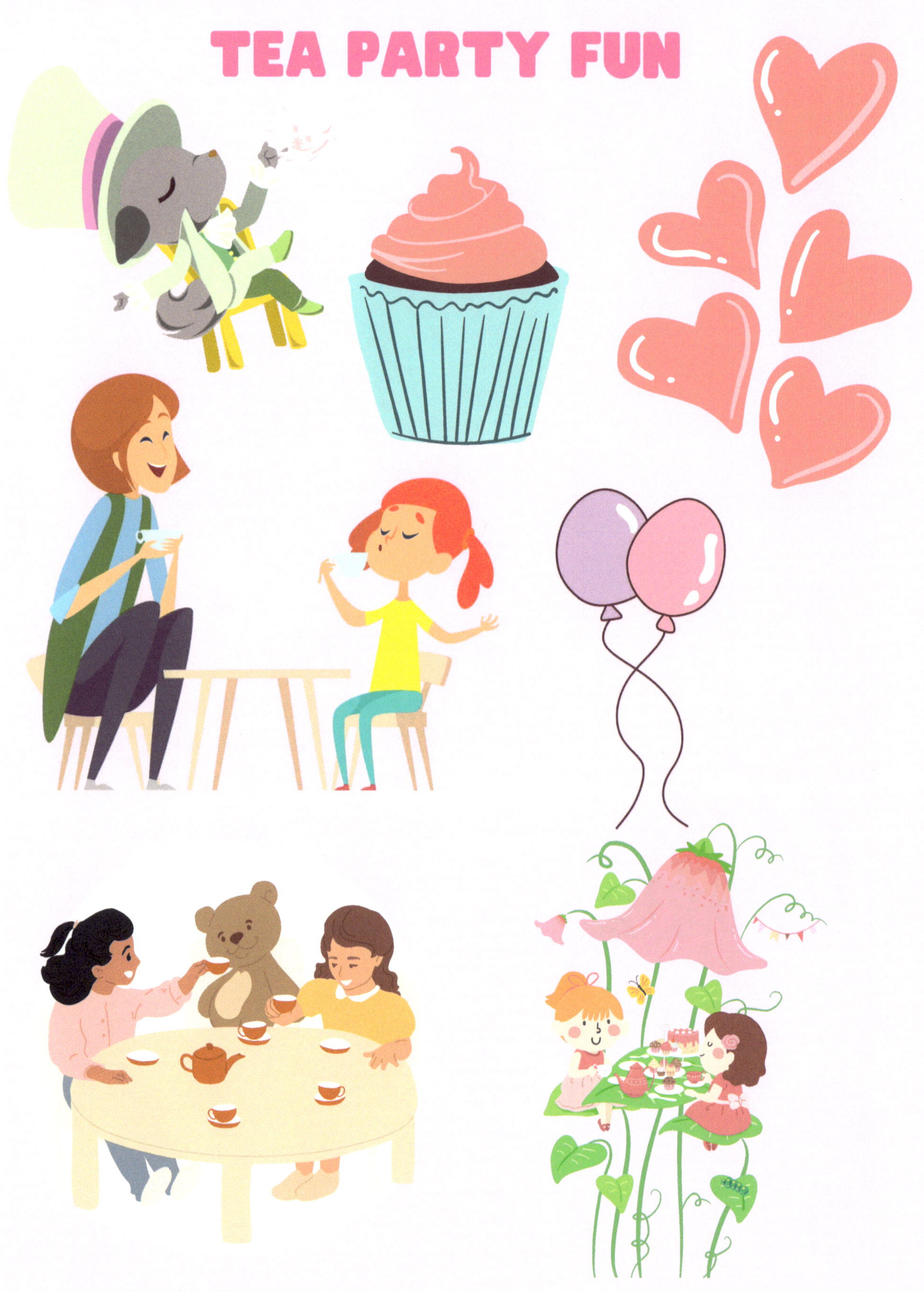

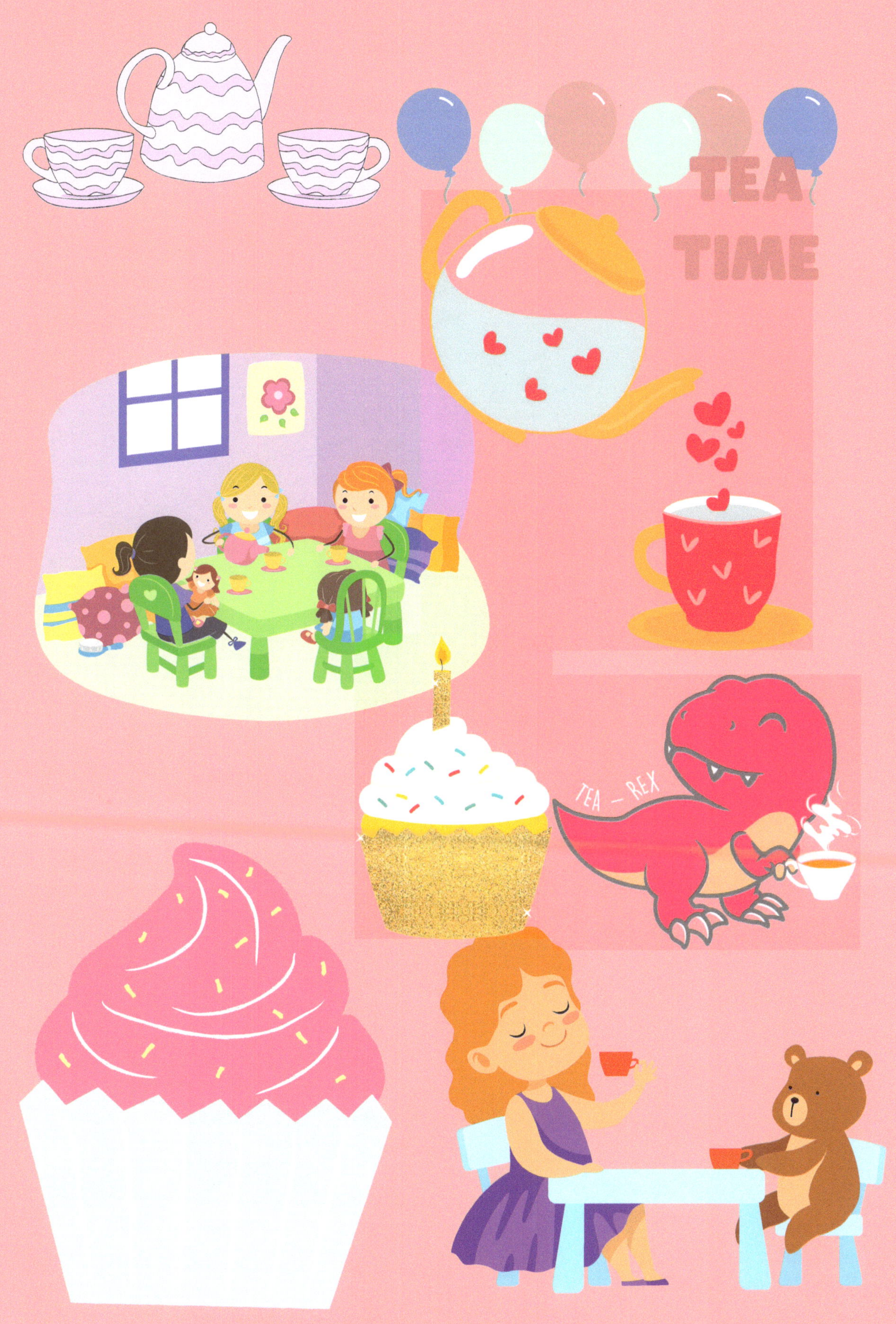
TEA
TIME
TEA - REX

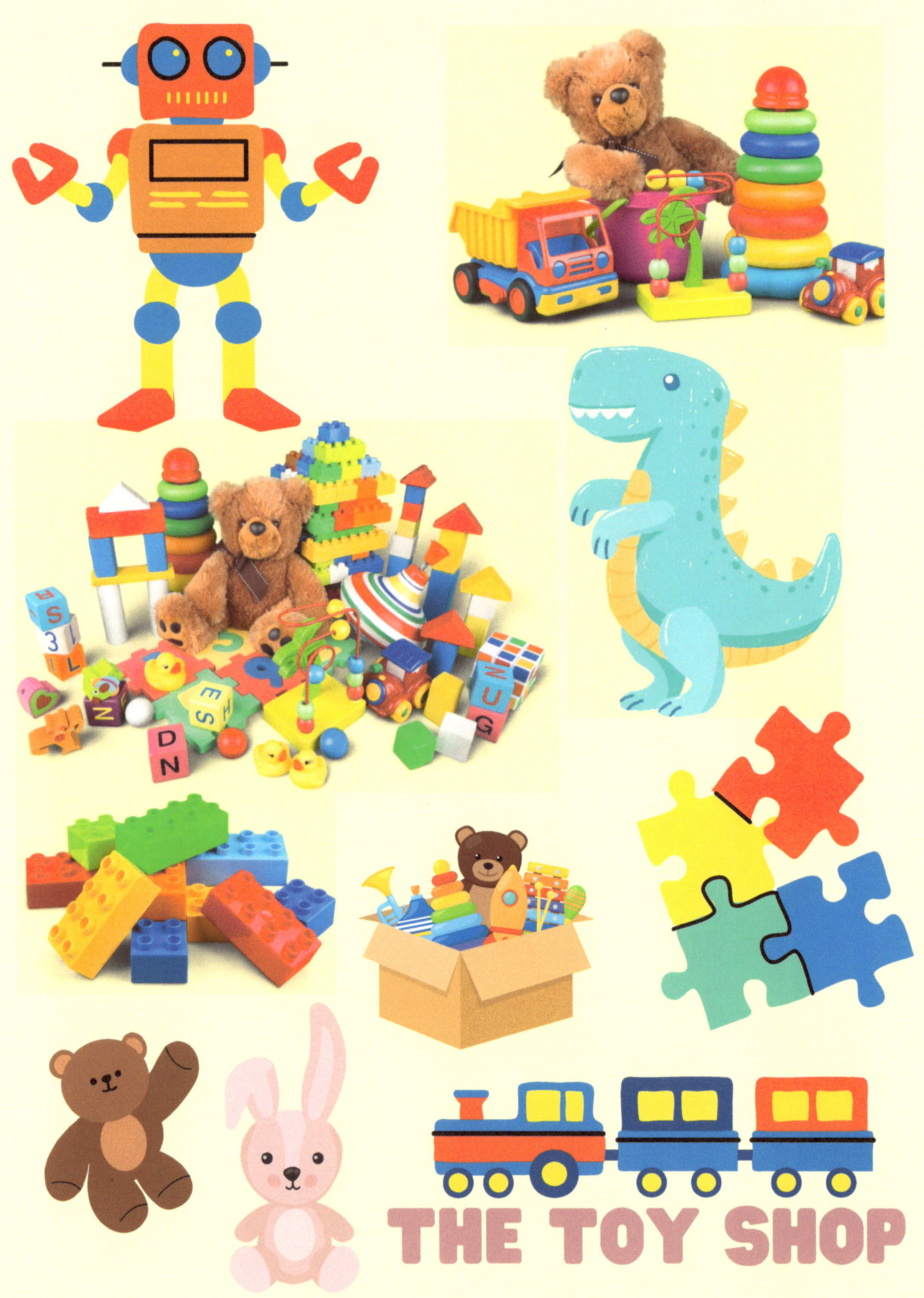

THE TOY SHOP

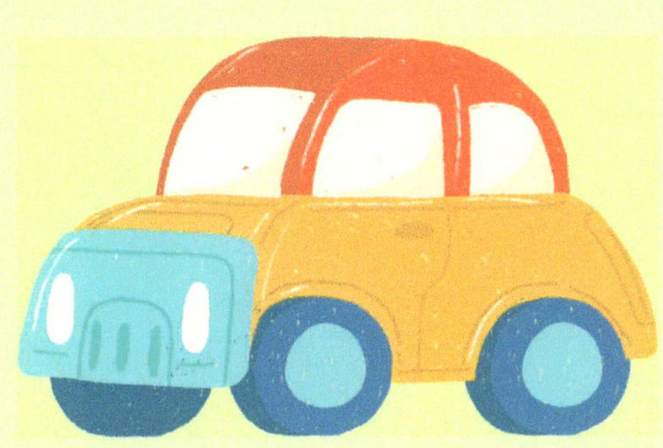

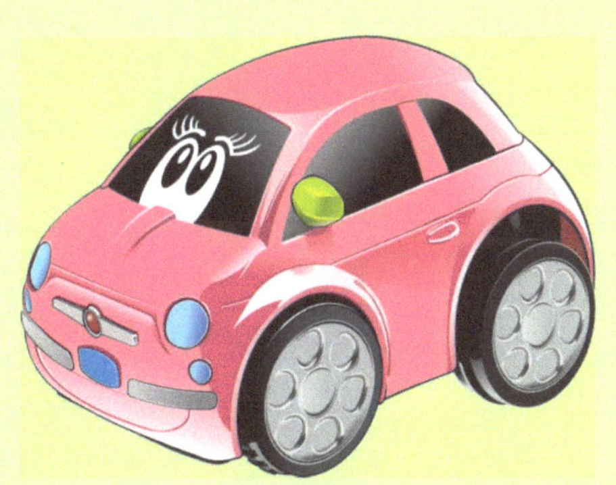

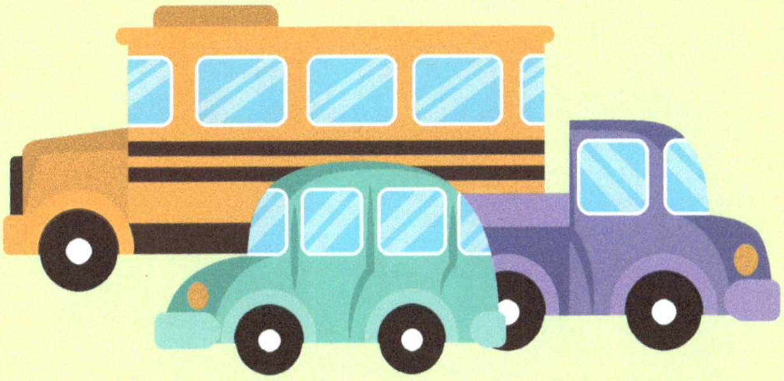

TRUCKS AND

CARS

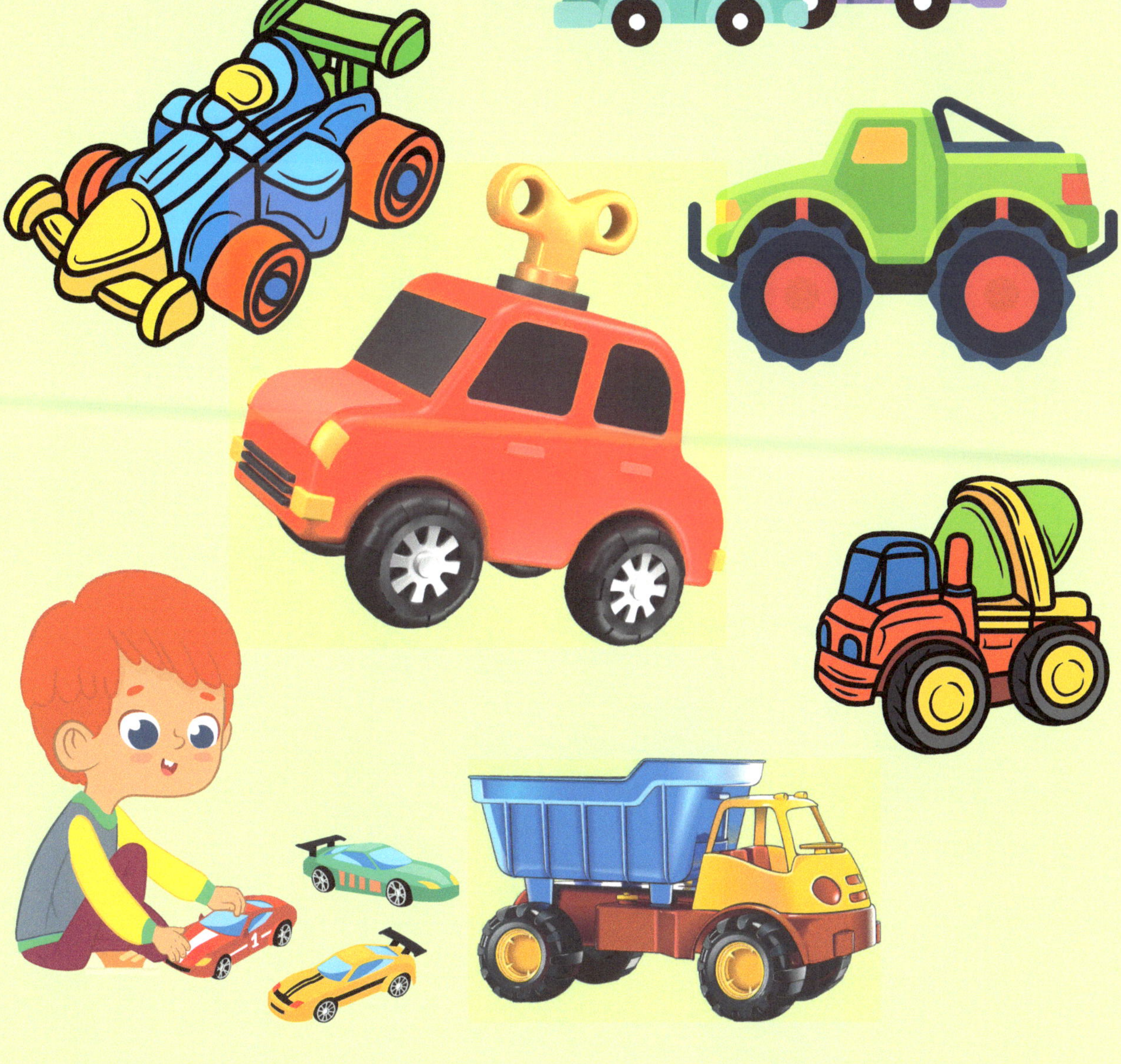

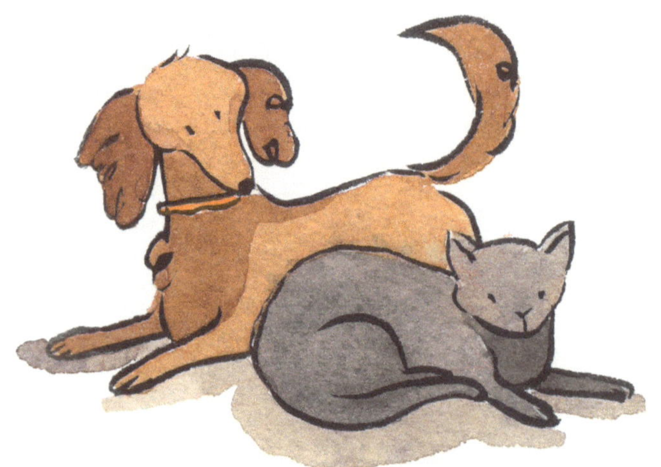

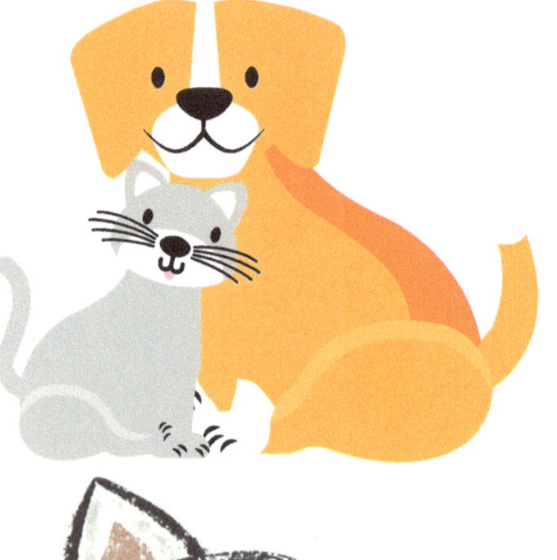

PET SHOP

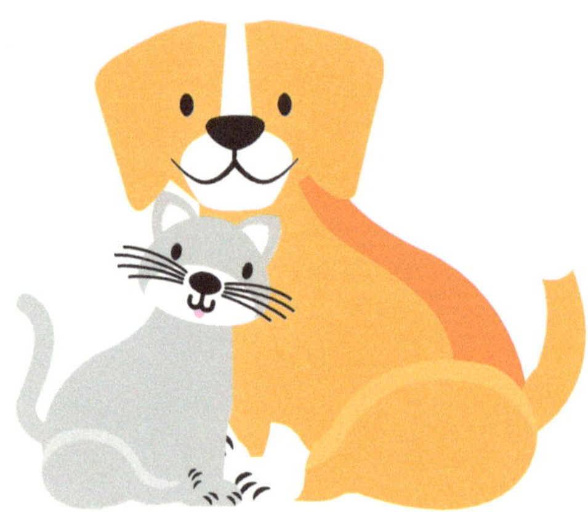

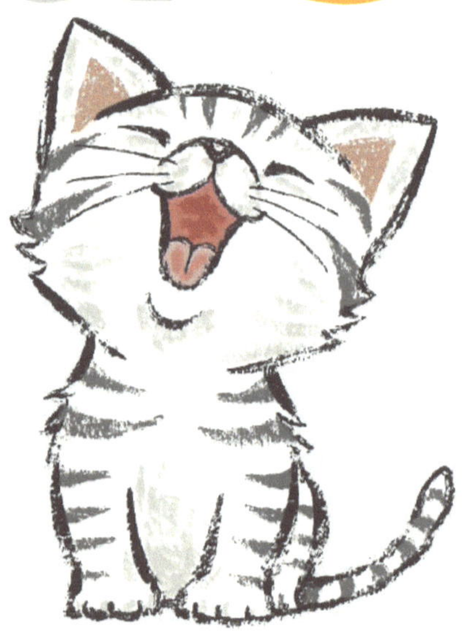

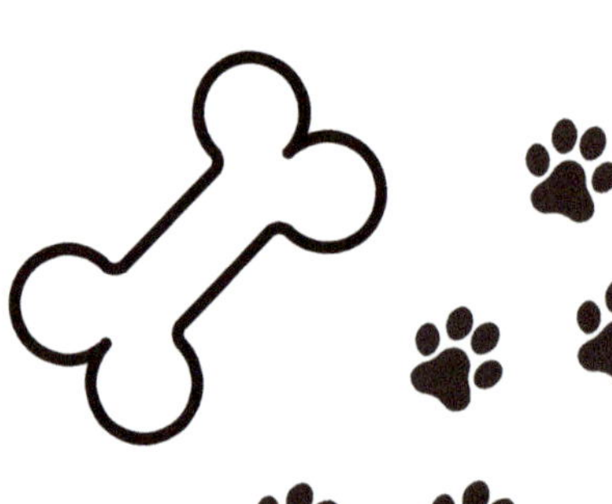

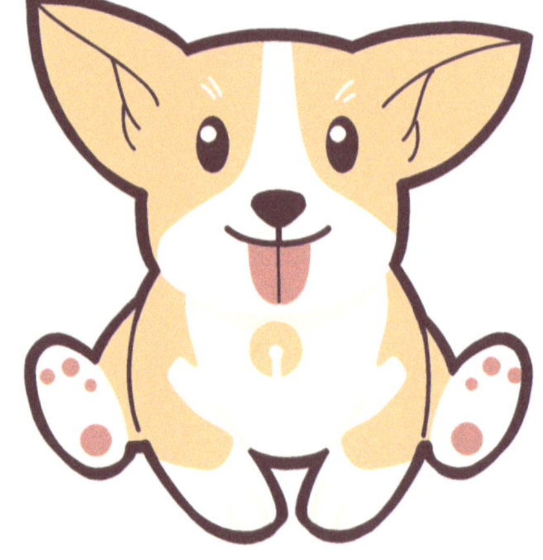

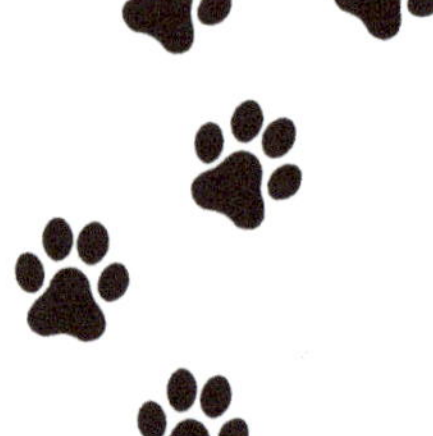

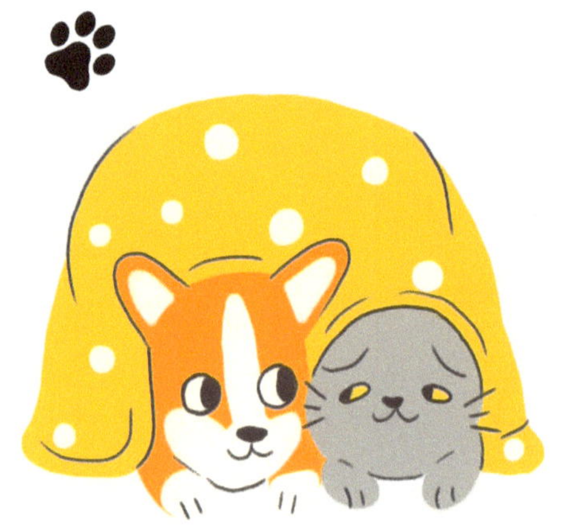

PETS

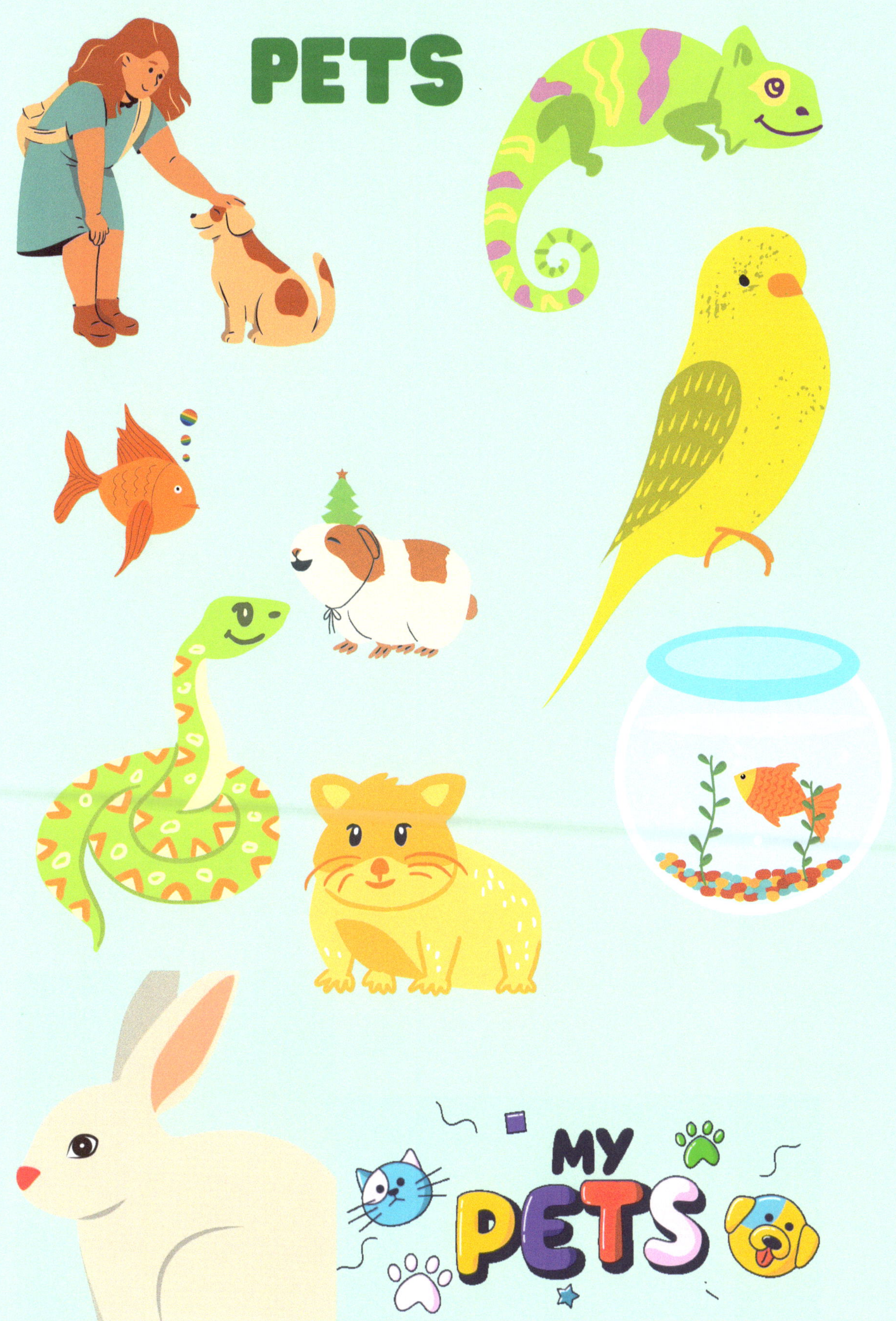

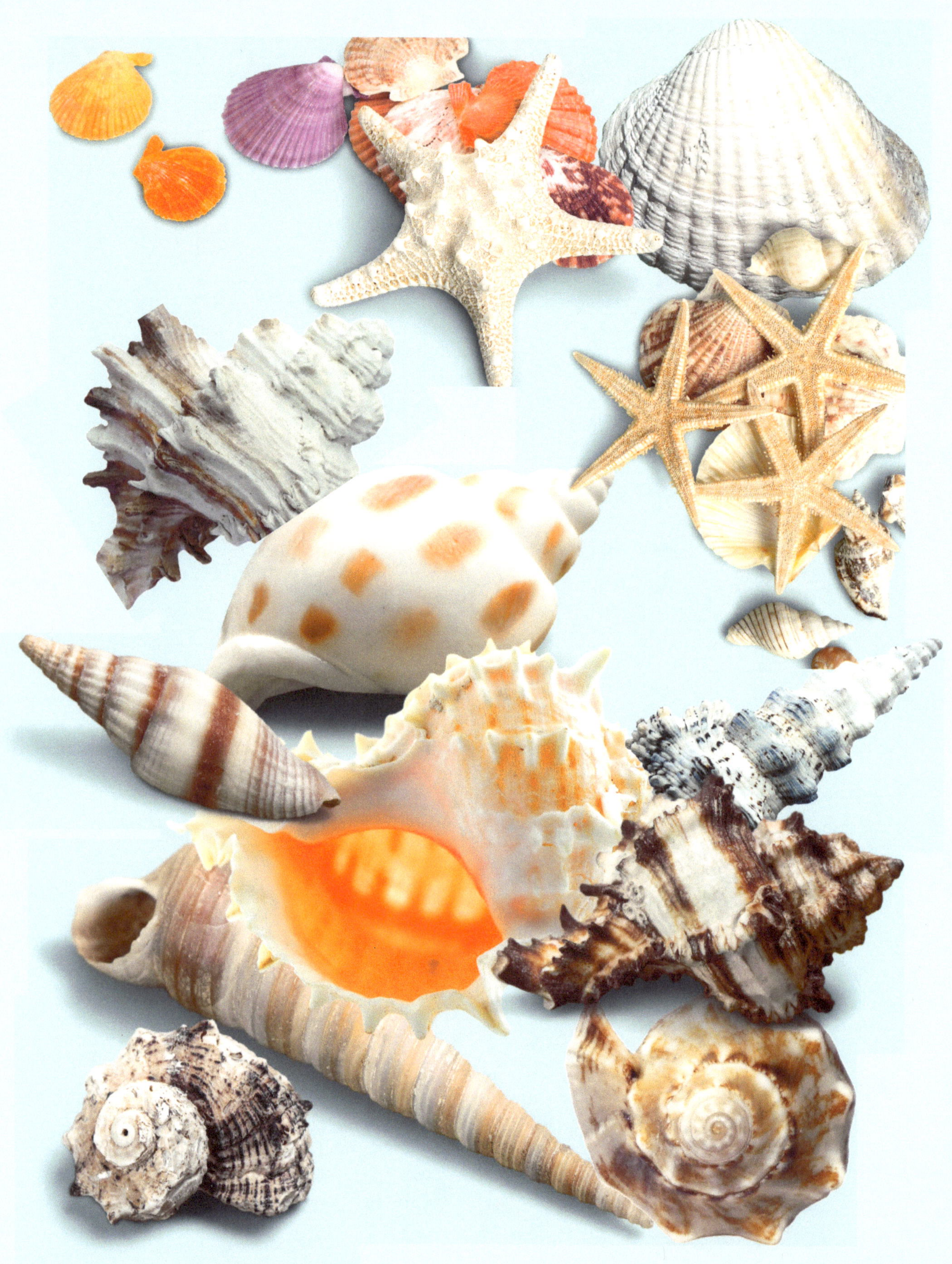

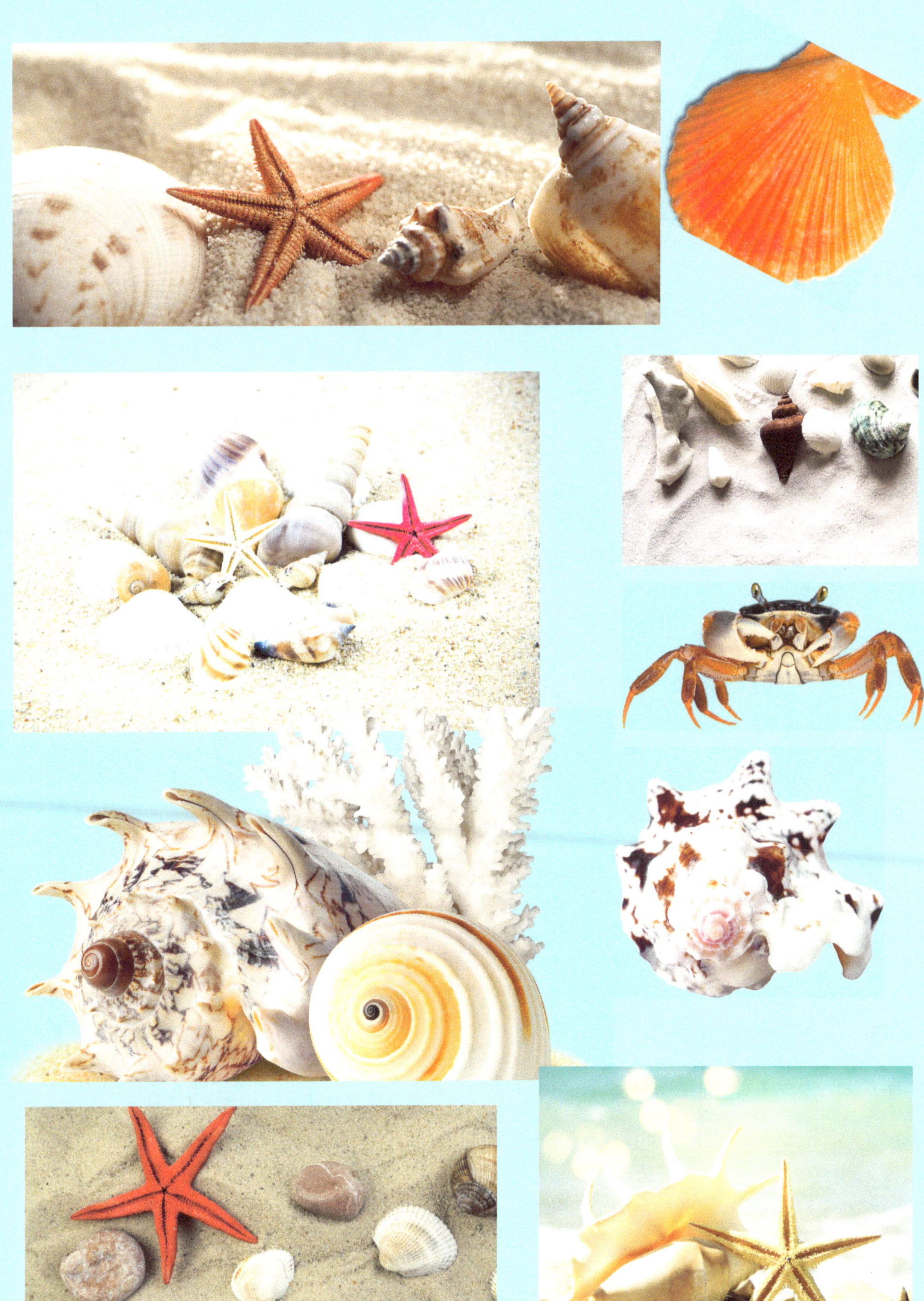

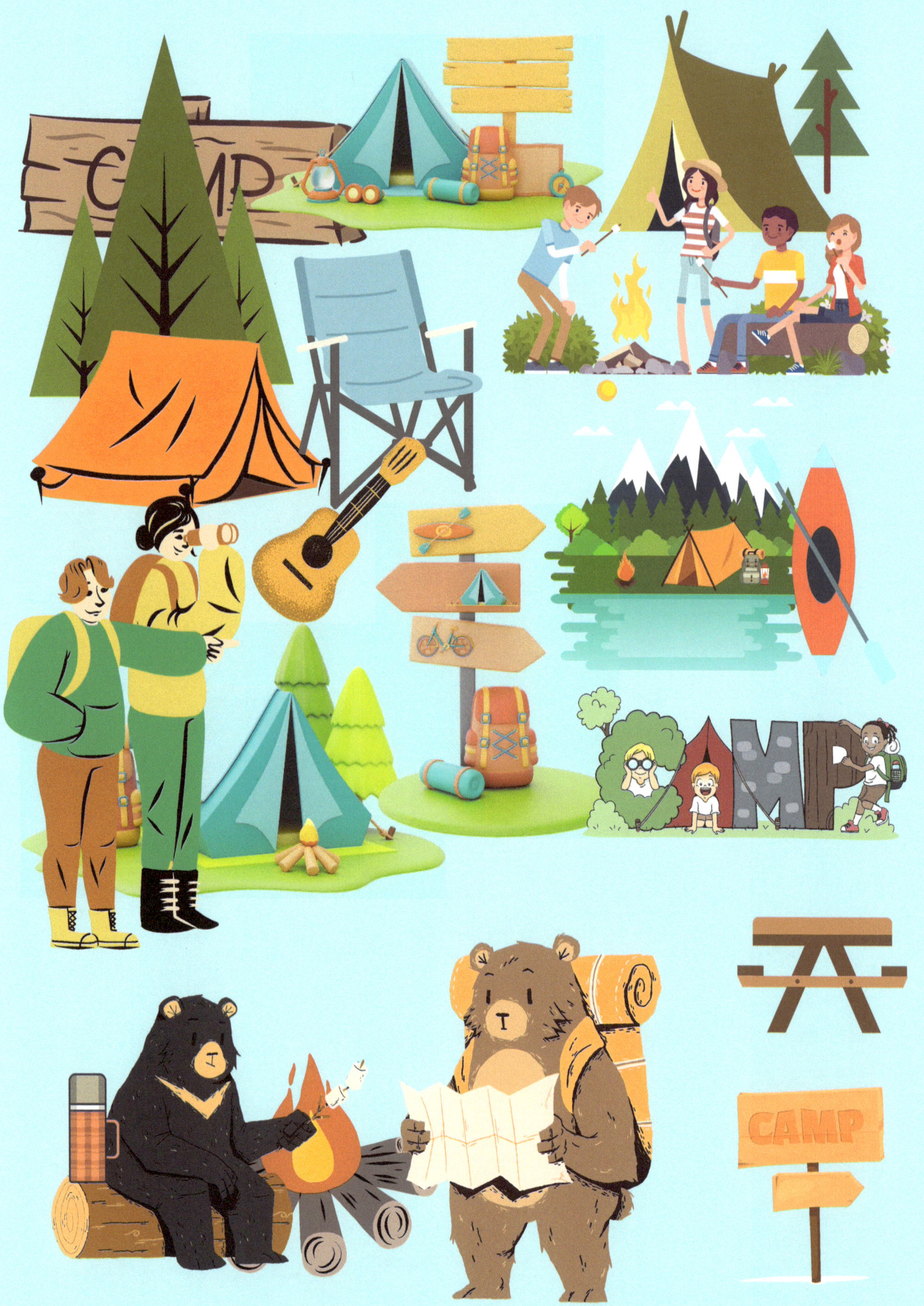

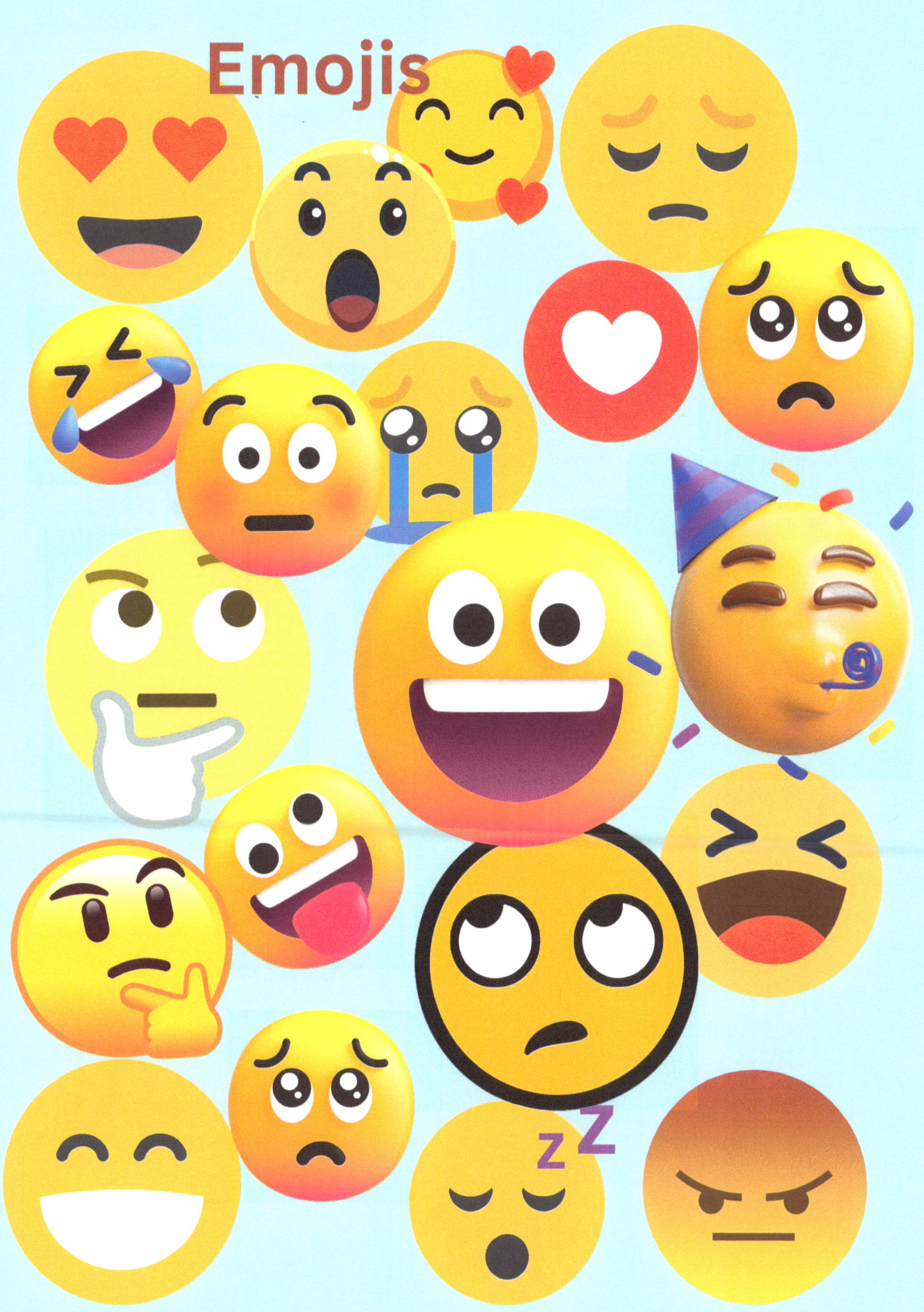

Emojis

Shapes

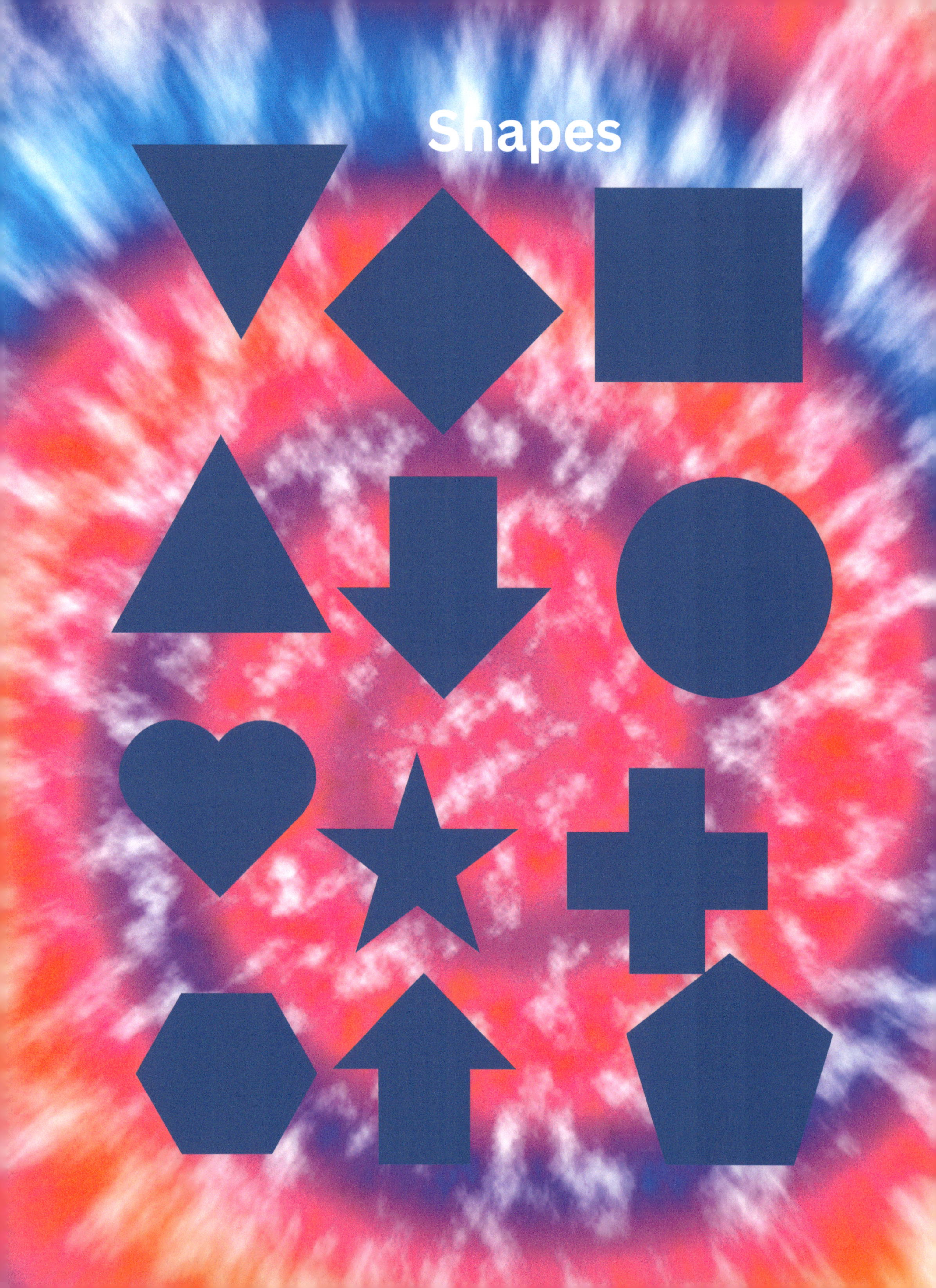

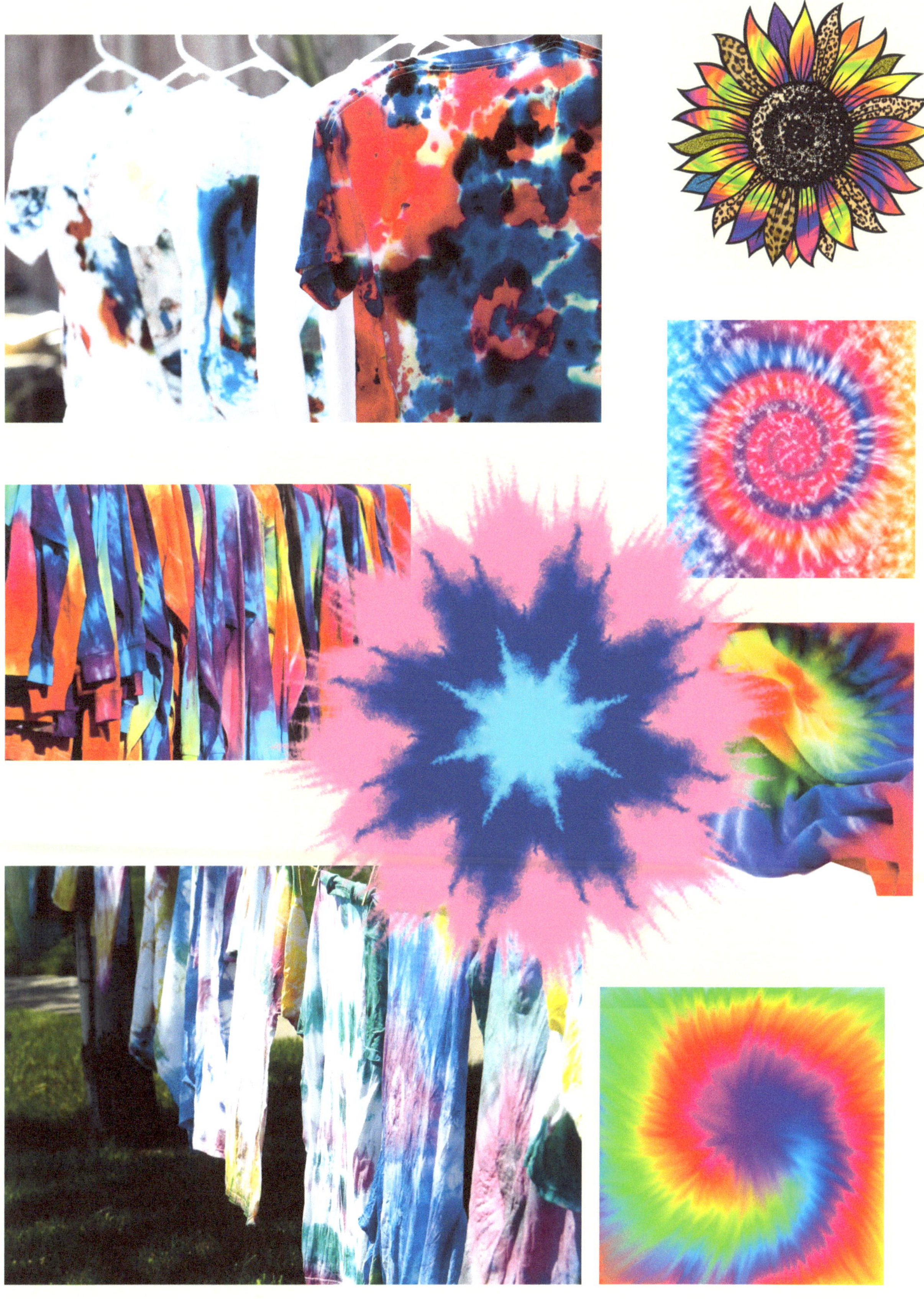

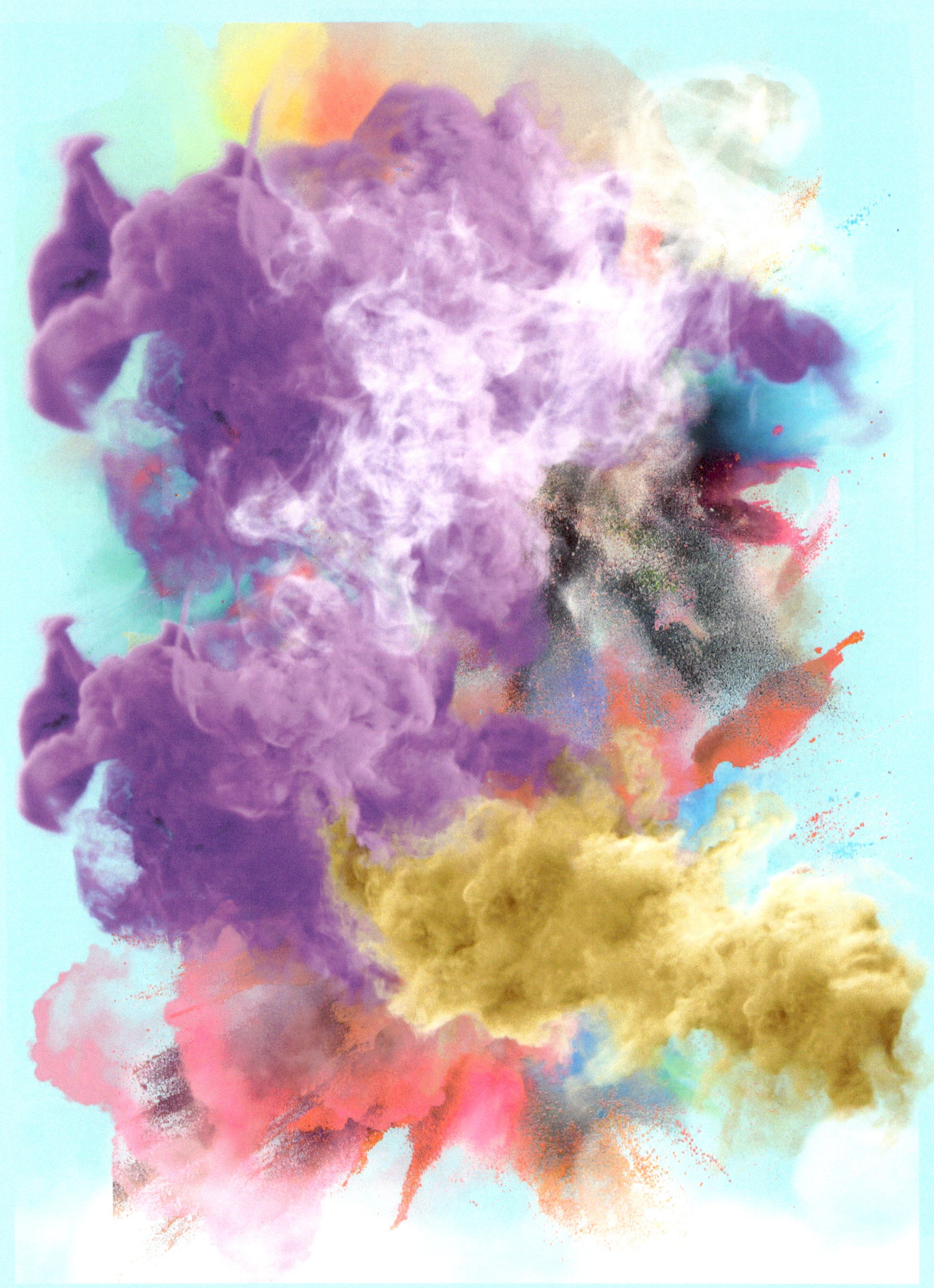

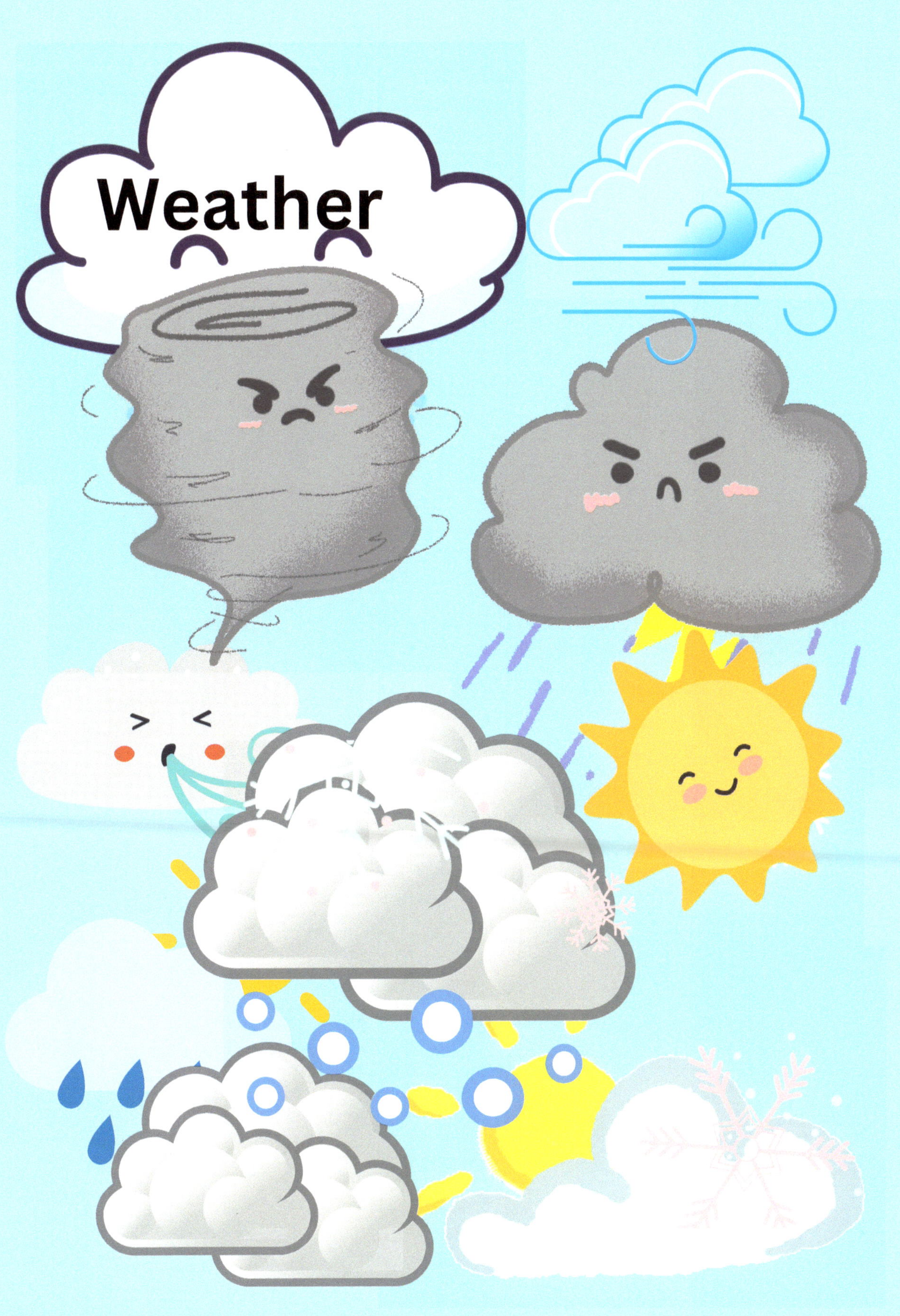
Weather

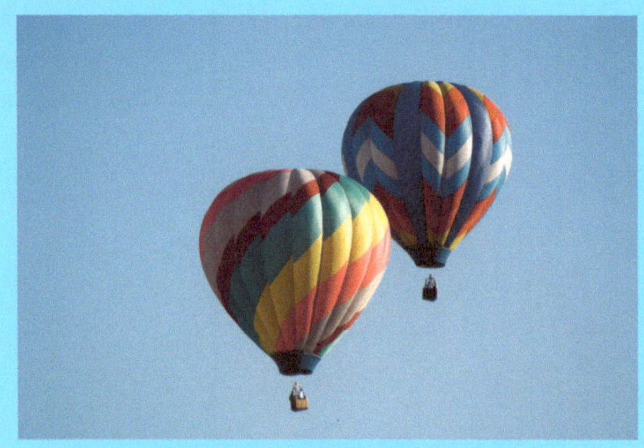
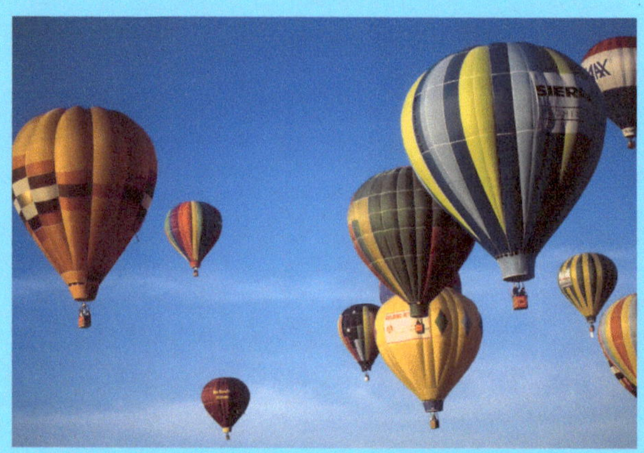
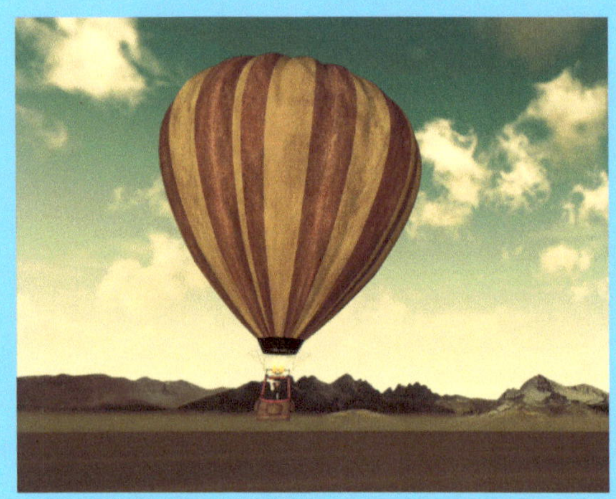
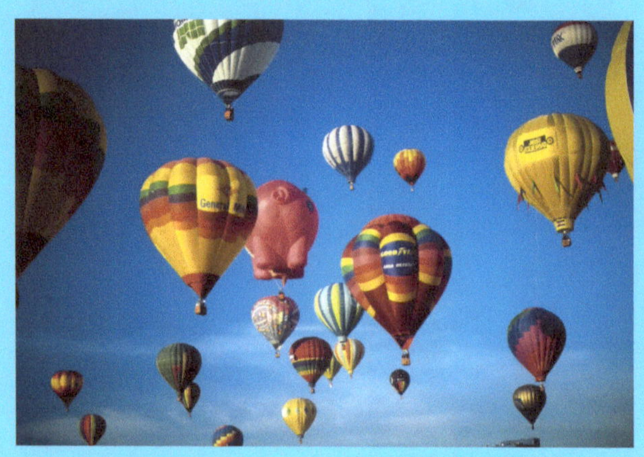
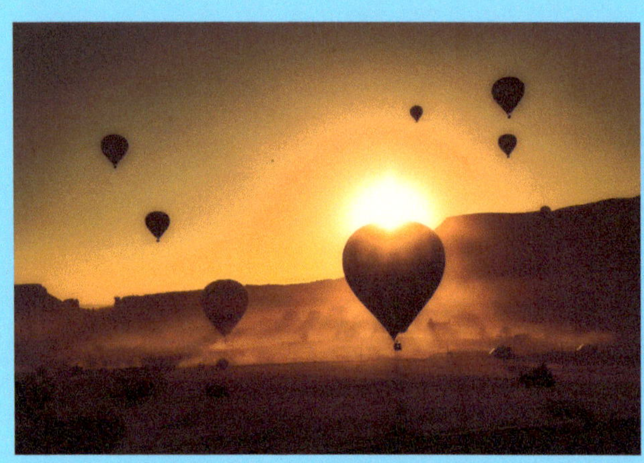
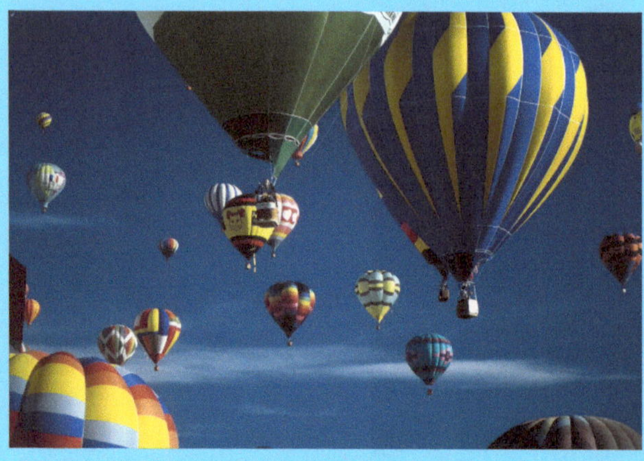

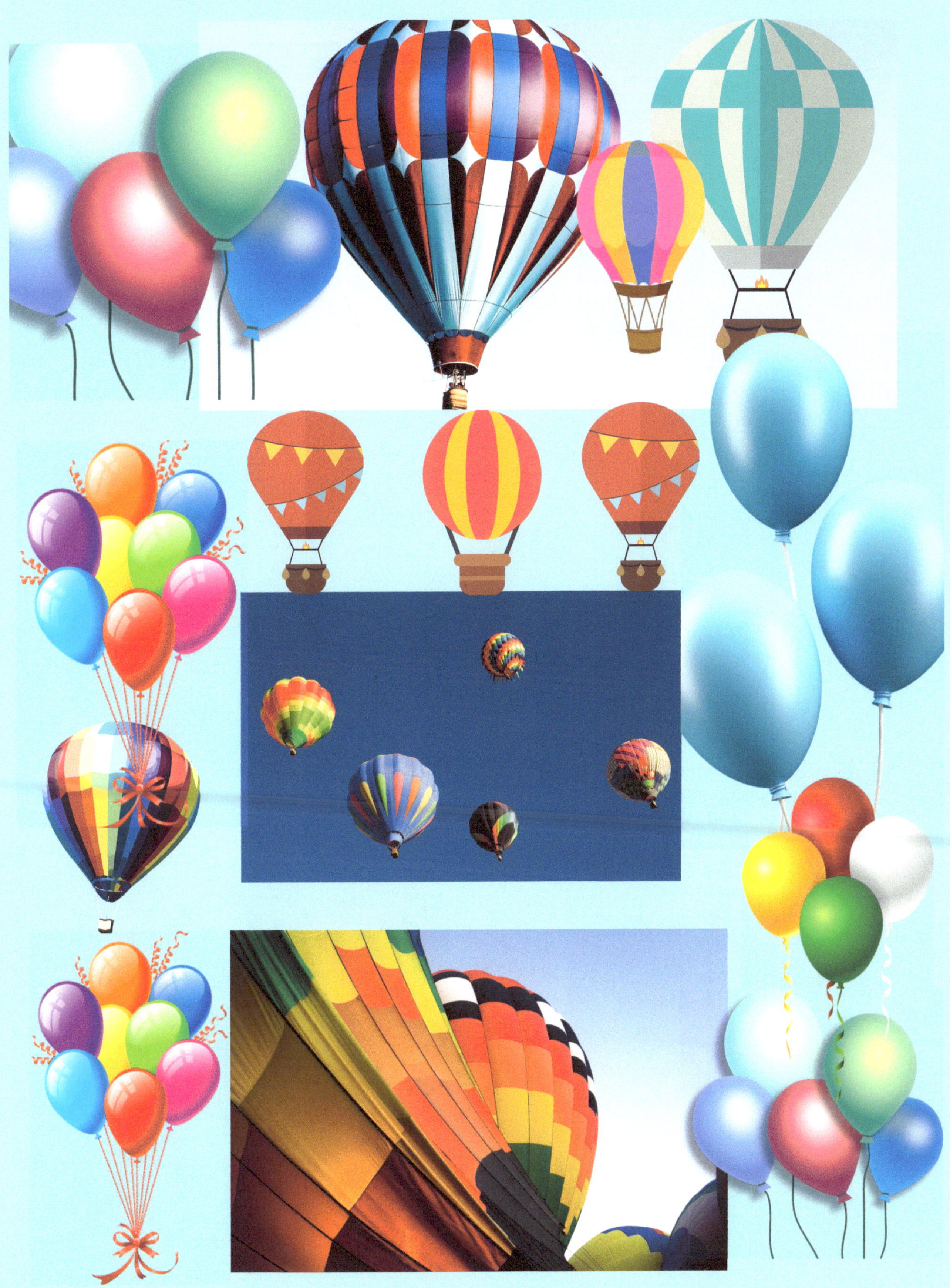

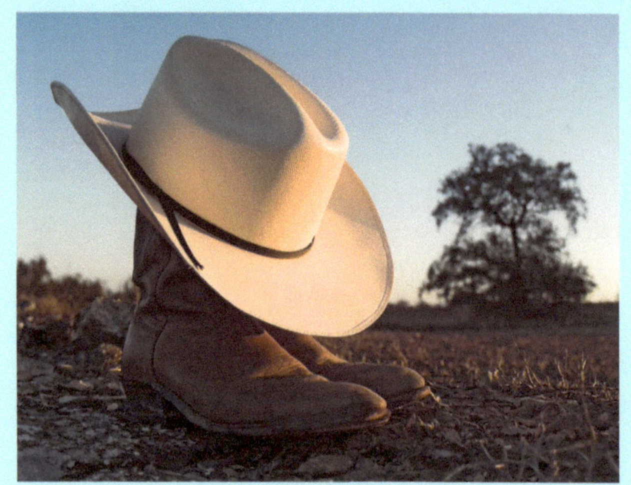
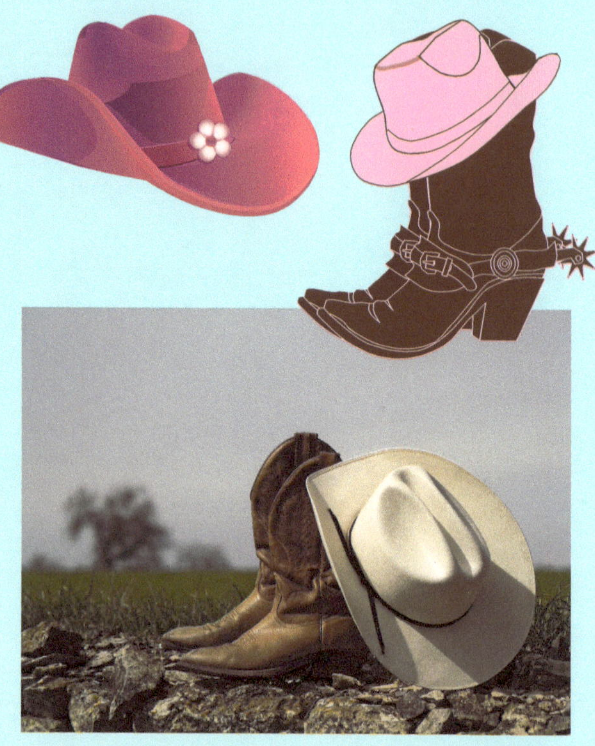
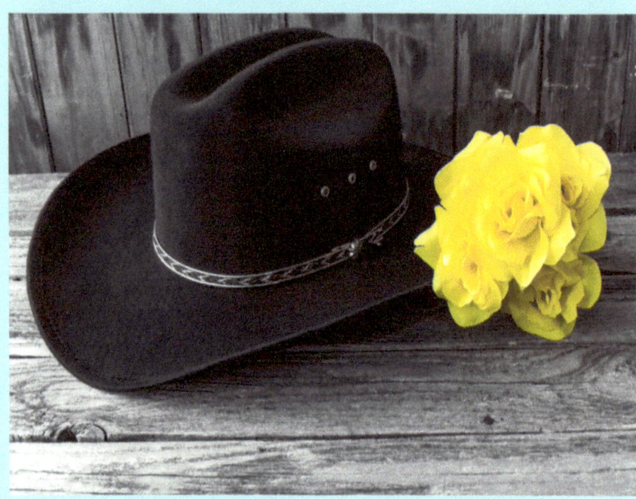
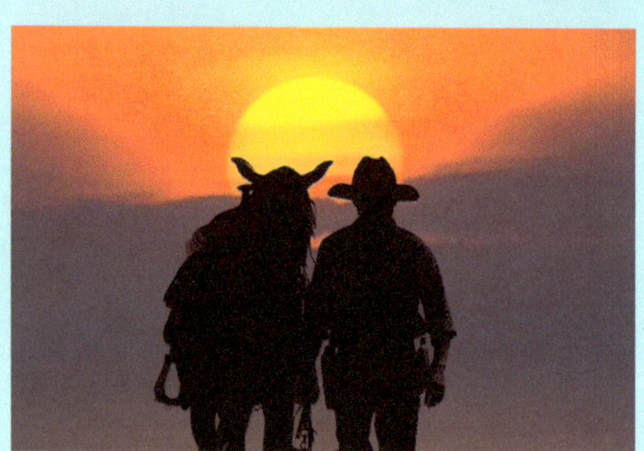
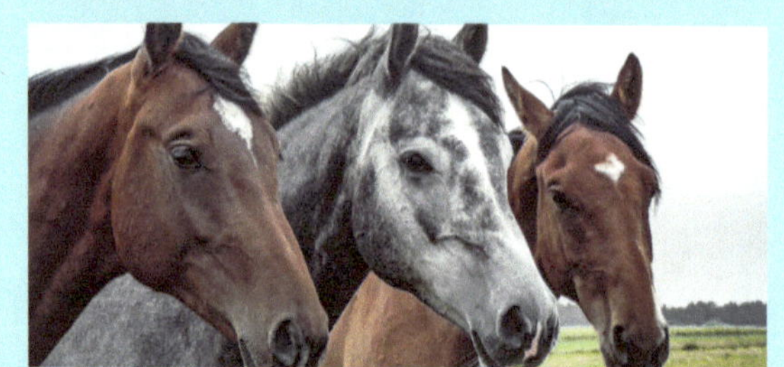
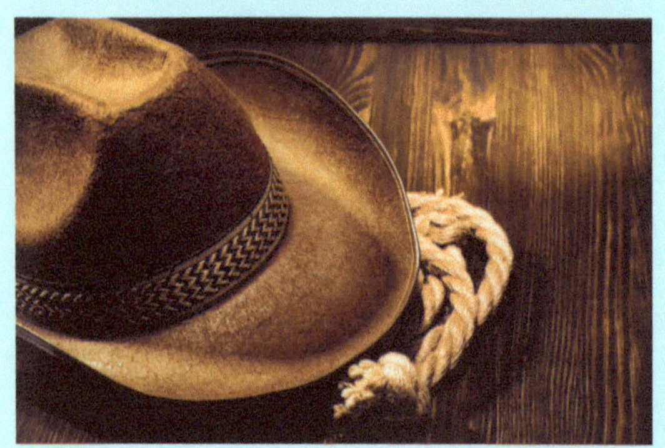
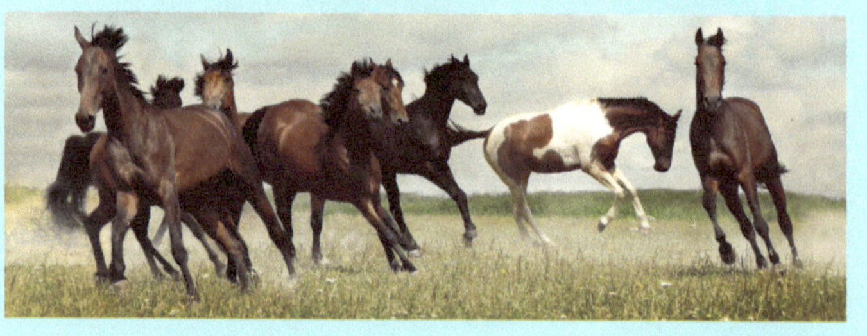
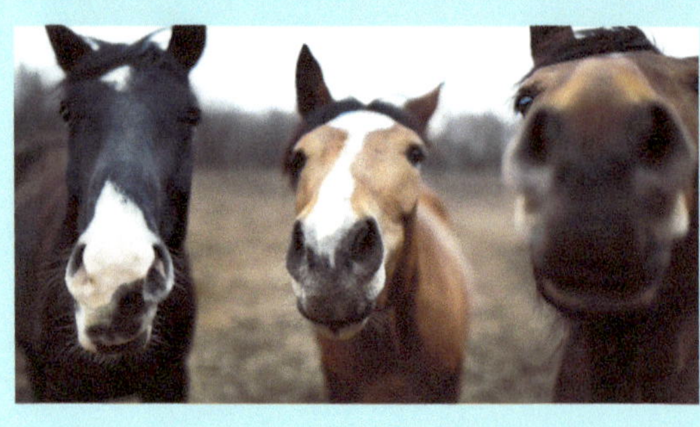

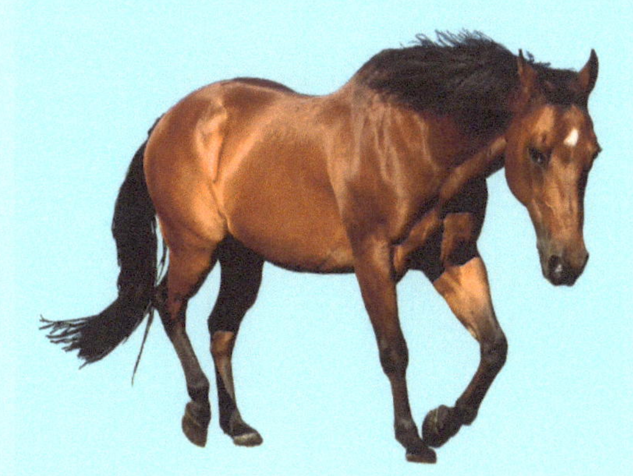
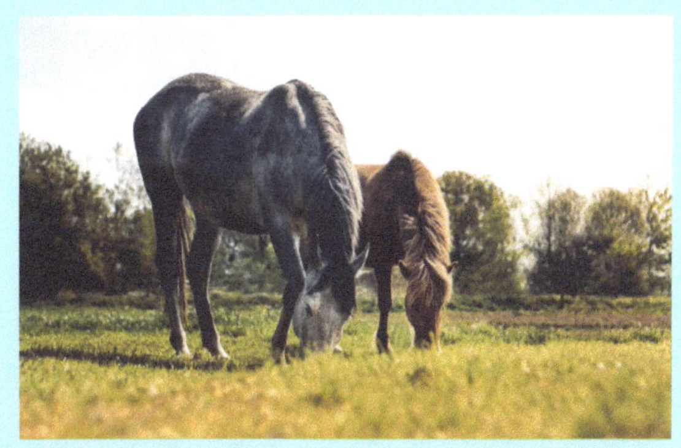
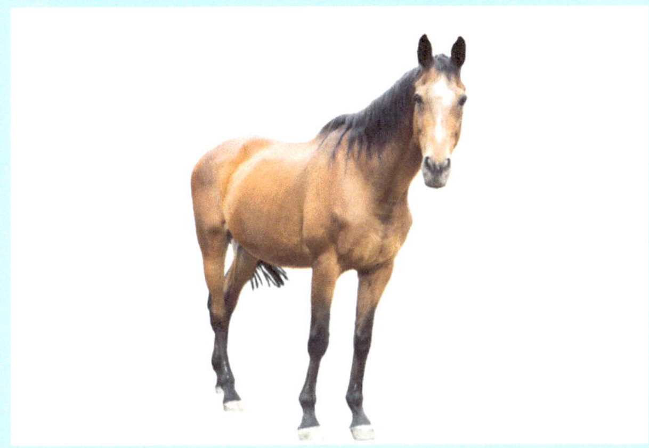
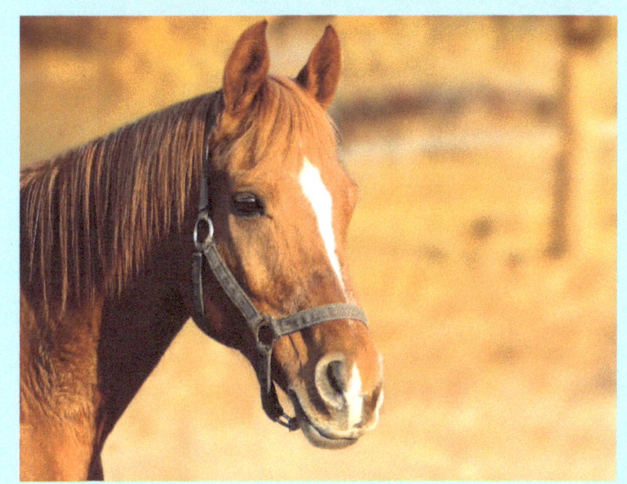
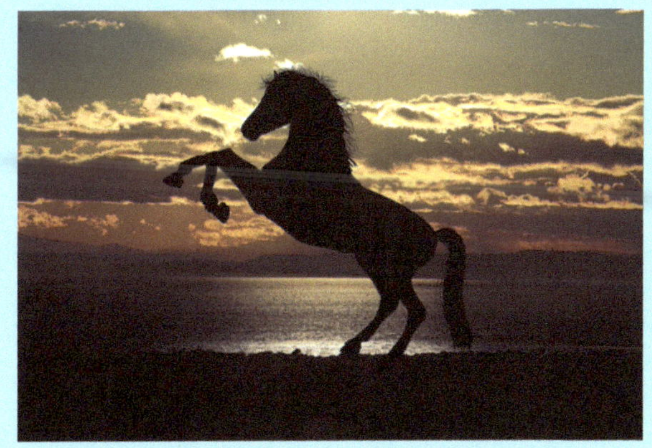
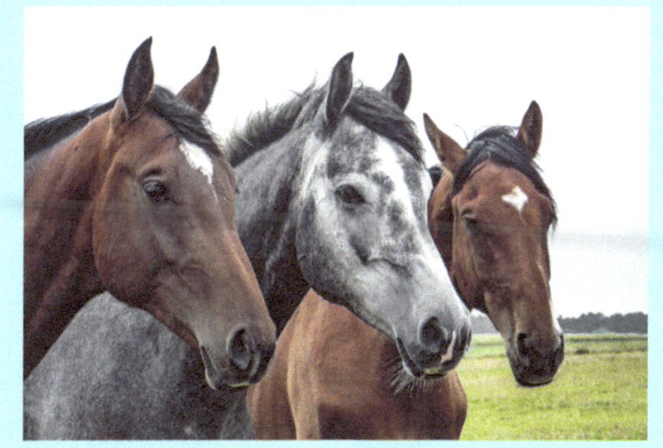
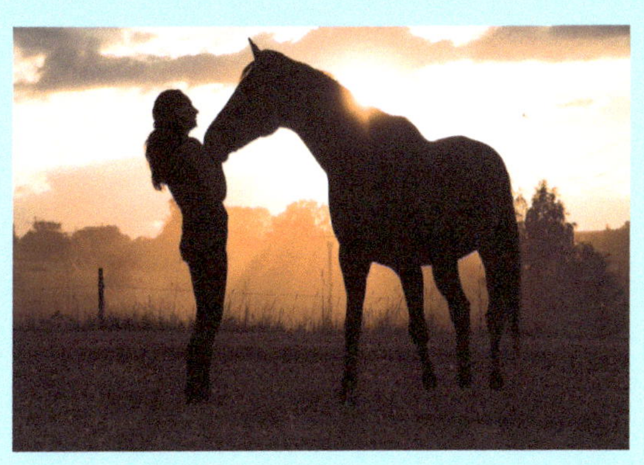
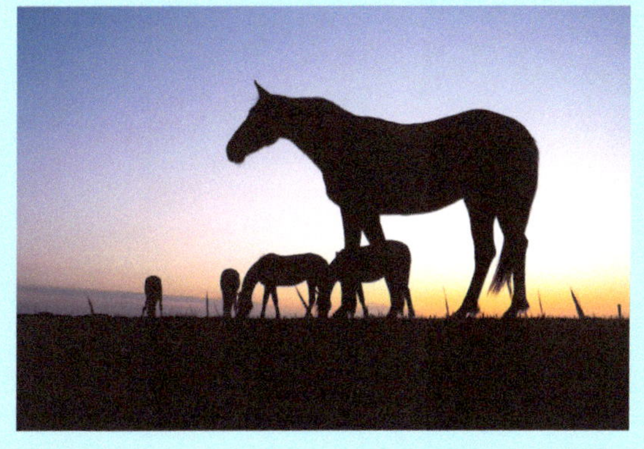

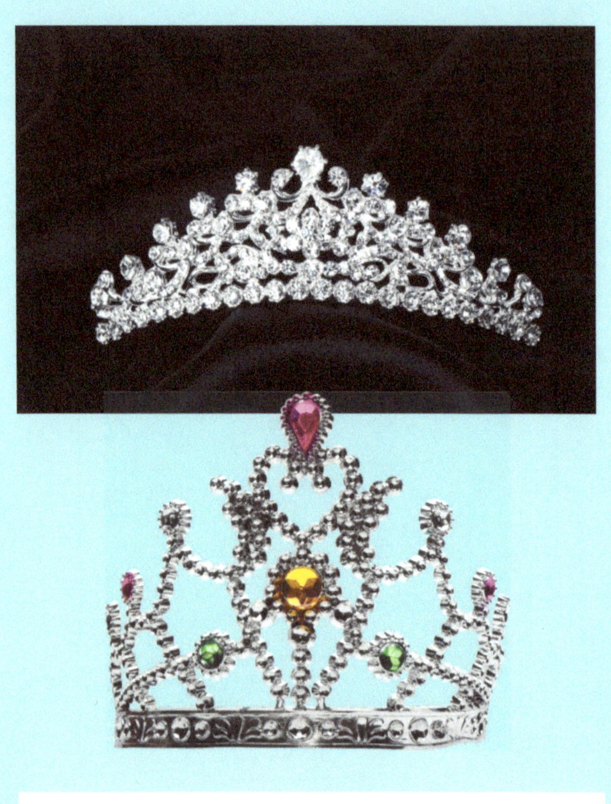

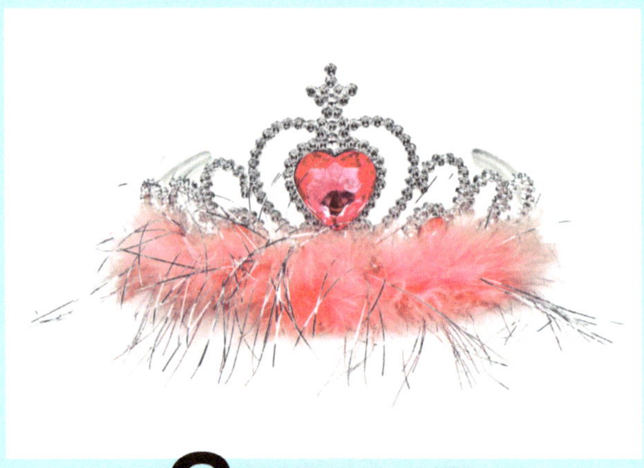

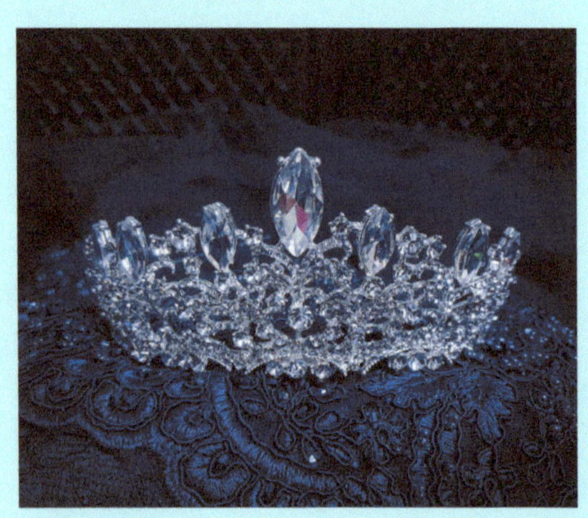

Crown

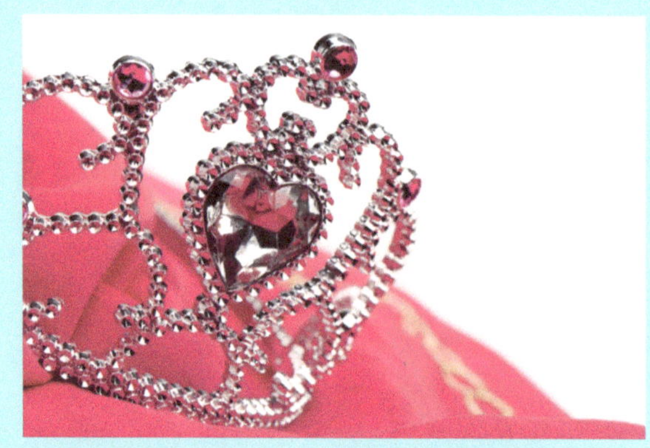

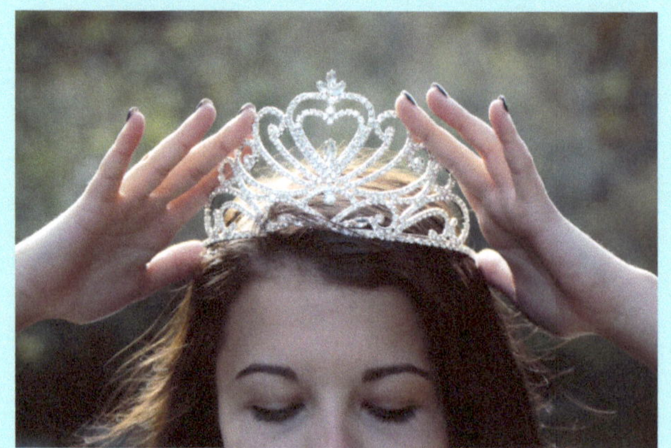

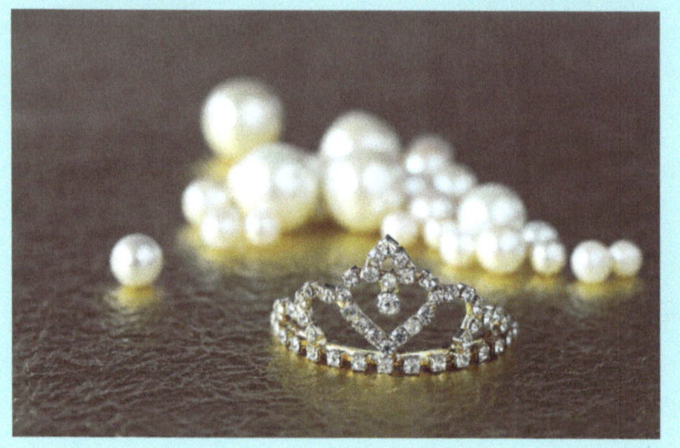

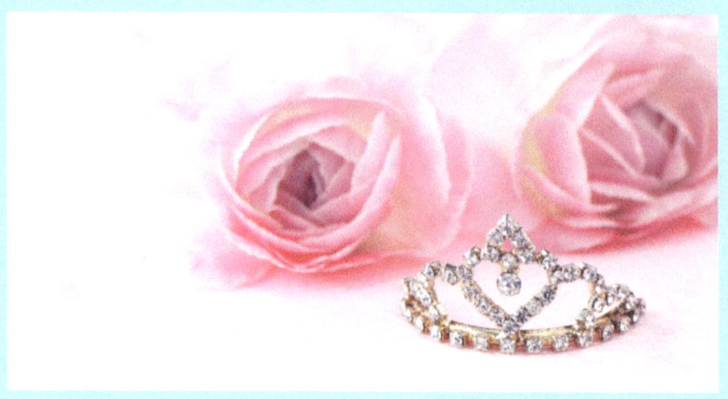

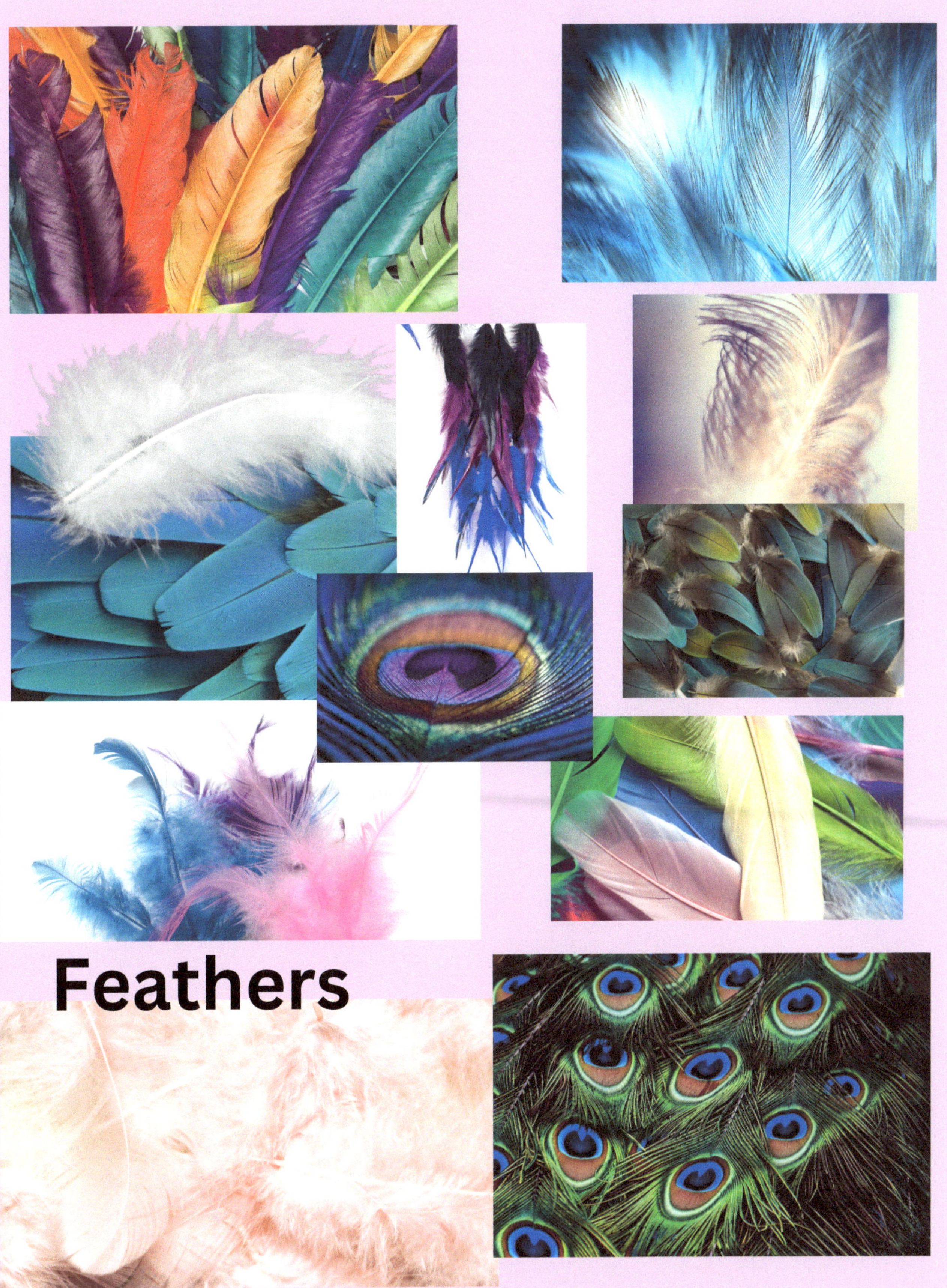

Feathers

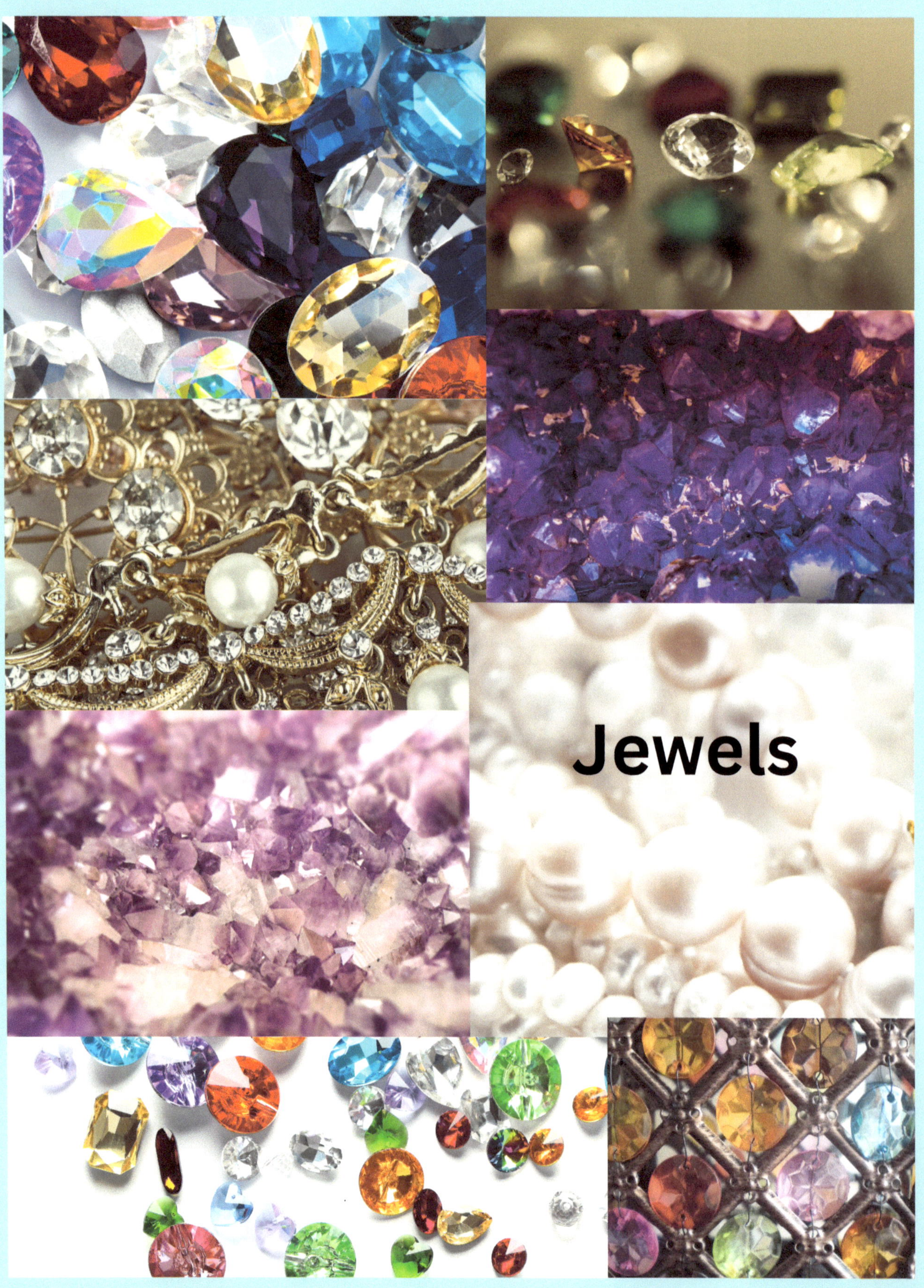
Jewels

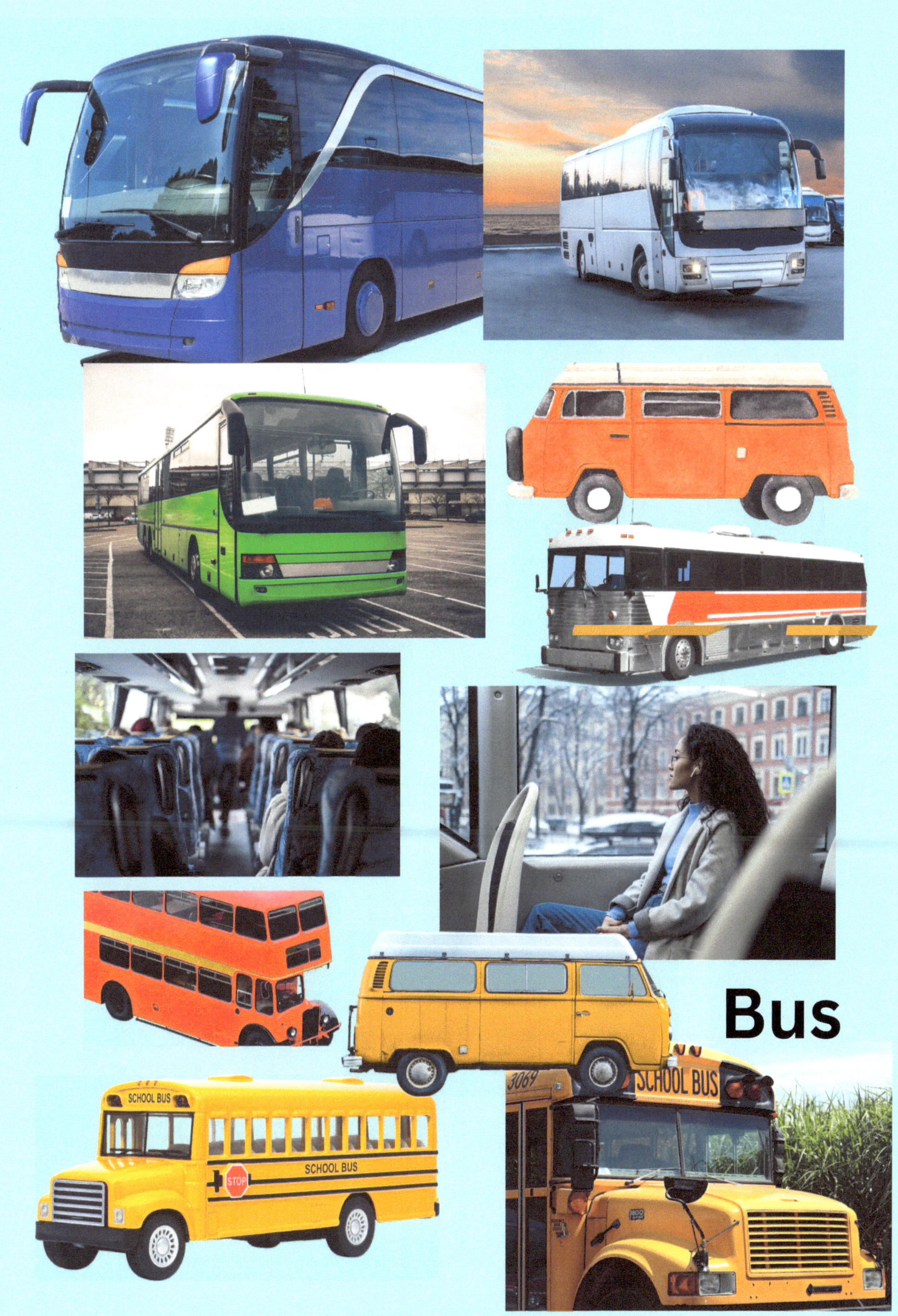

Bus

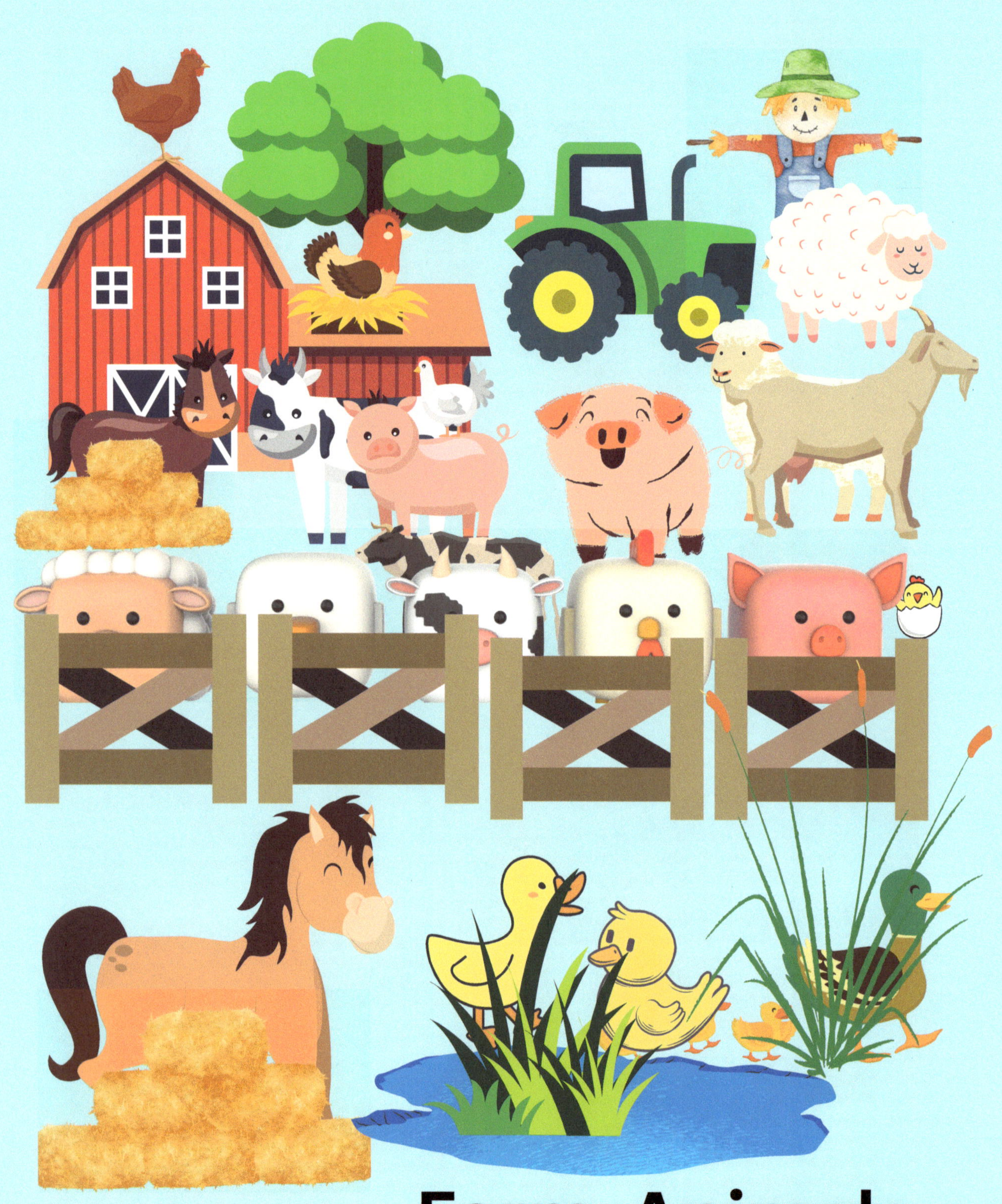

Farm Animals